Dr. Anna Mae Walsh Burke is presently a Director of Nova College of Nova University. Doctor Burke has designed a number of programs for the University and has long been involved with the needs of women who are returning to school. She has her Doctorate in Physics from Fordham University, over 50 technical and educational publications and is a member of a number of professional organizations. In addition, Dr. Burke has written children's books and is known locally for her water colors. Dr. Burke is married and has two children, ages 9 and 10. She has lived through many of the problems faced by the working and/or studying mother.

ARE
YOU
READY?

Anna Mae Walsh Burke

ARE YOU READY?

A Survival Manual
for Women Returning to School

A SPECTRUM BOOK

PRENTICE-HALL INC., Englewood Cliffs, New Jersey 07632

Library of Congress Cataloging in Publication Data

Burke, Anna Mae Walsh.
  Are you ready?

  (A Spectrum Book)
  Includes index.
    1. Education of women—United States—Handbooks,
  manuals, etc. 2. Study, method of—Handbooks,
  manuals, etc. 3. Continuing education—United
  States—Handbooks, manuals, etc. I. Title.
  LC1663.B87   376   80–15218
  ISBN 0–13–045617–9
  ISBN 0–13–045609–8 (pbk.)

© 1980 by Prentice-Hall, Inc., Englewood Cliffs, New Jersey 07632

A SPECTRUM BOOK

10 9 8 7 6 5 4 3 2 1

Printed in the United States of America

Prentice-Hall International, Inc., London
Prentice-Hall of Australia Pty. Limited, Sydney
Prentice-Hall of Canada, Ltd., Toronto
Prentice-Hall of India Private Limited, New Delhi
Prentice-Hall of Japan, Inc., Tokyo
Prentice-Hall of Southeast Asia Pte. Ltd., Singapore
Whitehall Books Limited, Wellington, New Zealand

To those who are my life and love
My parents, Nora and Peter
My husband, Bob
My children, Robert and Anna Mae

Contents

ARE
YOU
READY?

PART I

RETURNING: MAKING THE DECISION

chapter 1

Making the Decision

"YOU ARE NOT ALONE" is more than a caption for a science fiction film. It is a motto for women today. Although you may be involved or have definite feelings about what is called "the women's movement" this book is not about the movement or about your being part of that movement in any kind of formal sense. It is a book intended to help you, as an individual, to return to school. As the subtitle indicates, this book is also intended to be a manual for your survival once you have returned to the classroom.

RETURNING

What does the word returning mean to you? Is it a matter of coming back to a home or a time or a dream you once had? A famous author once said that you can't go home again, meaning that both home and you will have changed with time and things will not be the same. This is certainly true with respect to returning to school. You have been developing as a person, gaining certain skills, developing certain talents all your life. You may now be at a point where you are facing the prospect of making a major decision. If you are reading this book, the chances are that you are a woman who is thinking about returning to school. You may feel excited, scared, insecure. The thing you must *not* feel is alone.

You Are Not Alone

For the first and only time in this book, let's take a look at some numbers that will help you to realize why you should not feel alone. These figures, which were obtained from the Bureau of the Census, 1975, indicate the changes that have taken place in the college population since 1970. In the period from 1970 to 1976 there has been a 30 per cent increase in the number of women college students compared to men, whose numbers increased by only 12 per cent.[1]

The female college student population of 3,-898,000 in 1974 was 44 per cent of the total college population compared to 41 per cent in 1970. It is certain that the 1980 census will reveal that this trend has continued.

There is considerable interest in the "older" stu-

[1] Carol Kehr Tittle and Elenor Rubin Denker. "Re-entry Women: A Selective Review of the Education Process, Career Choice and Interest Measurement," *Review of Educational Research,* Vol. 47, 4, 1977, pp. 531–584.

dents who seem to be appearing with increasing frequency on the college campus. Collection of data was begun in 1972 on the over-35 age group. The percentage of change from 1970 to 1974 for college enrollments shows increases in all age groups but the 25–29 age group (108%) and the 30–34 (95%) age group showed impressive jumps. The over-35 group showed a 32 per cent gain in the school year 1973–1974 alone. The number of women in the over-35 age group outnumbers the men. These figures do not include those who attend the adult education type of classes. As you can see, you are not alone. You will be one of four million!

As the director of the undergraduate education programs in a major university, I developed a program in teacher education for women (primarily) who are returning to school. This program has been phenomenally successful. In its first 2½ years of operation, it has served the needs of over a thousand students 95 per cent of them women.

These women came from a variety of backgrounds. Some had come from disadvantaged educational backgrounds and had never hoped to have the opportunity to go back to school. Others had begun college before they were married and had dropped out for any one of a number of reasons. Some were in desperate economic conditions, whereas others had substantial family incomes. All were excited, and all were motivated to a degree that impressed their teachers, many of whom had survived the students of the late 1960s and early 1970s. All had problems juggling time and learning to do new things. Many had problems with basic skills, with writing papers, and with doing library research. Some had problems financing their education, others had prob-

lems getting their families to understand and participate in the new demands that resulted because of
their going back to school. In spite of this, many completed their program, and I was as proud as they
when I handed them their diplomas as they walked
across the stage at graduation. Graduation was itself
a family affair, and several students who are now
teaching in their own classrooms tell me they often
thought they would never make it. "That's my Mom!"
was the theme of posters and cheers at the 1979 graduation.

This book is intended to help you to meet the
same problems and to gain the skills needed for returning to college. The women described earlier had
the added experience of being in a program designed
for them. They did not have to accommodate themselves to a program designed for students just out
of high school. This book also approaches the problem of the "returnee." How do you act, how do you
dress, what do you talk about if you are the only
returnee in a class of young people?

Why Women Return to School

Women return to school for a number of reasons.
Some return because they want to add another dimension to their lives, they want to develop themselves further. They seek additional interests, or they
have interests that they wish to follow. Some return
to school because they have always wanted to finish
their education.

Other students see a direct relationship between
employment and education. A college degree and,
in recent years, an advanced degree, have become
the prerequisite for a "good" job and advancement

in many areas. Many women are already working and are preparing for "better" jobs. The jobs may be "better" in terms of pay or in terms of self-fulfillment and satisfaction. Others are looking toward the day when they may or must join the work force. Many women must work. Some are married but many are divorced, widowed or separated. Some may never have married. Some are "separated" in thought and action from their husbands even though they are living in the same household. Others are supported and encouraged by their husbands and children in both their studies and their plans. Many work because the money is needed for the support of their families. The high rate of inflation is having a tremendous effect on the women in the nation's work force. Money spent on education may, indeed, be a good investment considering today's economic picture. It certainly is a good personal investment. If you are going to make this investment of yourself, your time, your family involvement and your money in an educational program you must plan carefully. You are planning your future; you are planning your Return.

chapter 2

Getting Your ideas and Yourself Together

DECIDING TO RETURN TO SCHOOL

It is said that the best time to buy anything is last year. The best time to have done something to change your life pattern might also have been last year— or the year before or ten or twenty years ago. Rule one must be established at this point. DON'T GET SO DISCOURAGED THAT YOU STOP. Write it down on a piece of paper, paint it on a rock, or embroider it on your crying towel or security blanket.

You can expect to get discouraged at times. Everyone does. The important thing is not to stop planning and working toward your goals when you do get discouraged. Whatever you do, don't stop before you start.

You may catch yourself saying, "It will take too long," "I don't have the time," "I can't do it," "I'll wait until after————." Don't fill in your favorite excuse. Think positively, especially when you think about yourself.

Time flies and sometimes hopes and dreams fly with it. Perhaps last year (or that other time) was not the best time to do something. The best time may be now. You have reached a level of maturity. You have had a number of life experiences. You are not the person you were last year. You are different and what is right for you will be different. Think of the time that has passed since you were last in school as a valuable learning experience.

Think of yourself in positive terms. Your life is good. What can you do to make your life more satisfying? Returning to school will certainly add a new dimension to your days. It will be an exciting and rewarding experience. It may not always be easy. There will be new demands on yourself, on your time, your life and your family. There will be many decisions to make.

The Cinderella story does not happen to many of us. Most of us have to work at making our dreams come true. There is no magic wand to take us from our urban or suburban fireside as it took the hardworking, unloved Cinderella to a world of dreams. The magic lies within each of us to direct our own dreams. It is up to us to release that magic.

Making Plans

If you are going to change your life in any way you must prepare a blueprint for that change. The task I am going to ask you to perform will be useful in drawing up your blueprint.

Find a time when you will not be interrupted, take a pad of paper and a pen, and find your favorite place to sit. You may not be able to finish this in one sitting. After all it is your life you are planning!

Begin by making a list of "Class One" dreams. If you could do or be anything in the world—with no constraints—what would you be? Forget about lack of money, talent, time and education. Disregard constraints of family or present life-style. This is your mental and emotional getaway list.

Next I want you to refine this list of dreams and eliminate those which have virtually no potential for actually coming true. Eliminate those items for which you have absolutely no talent or "historic" possibility of achivement. Do *not* eliminate those for which you lack training or education. You are trying to add a new dimension to your life. Let your imagination go free.

The next step is to add to your list. Begin with those activities or educational opportunities which are appealing to you and which have more potential for realization than the selections already eliminated from your original list. After you have written down the things you can immediately think of, you may want to supplement the list in some way. If you are not very excited by the items which remain, try to investigate further opportunities by looking at the selection of materials on careers at your local library. College catalogues can also be a source of ideas and will be discussed in a later section. The Dictionary of Occupational Titles produced by the Department of Labor lists thousands of jobs, many of which you may never have heard of. Counselors at local colleges may be able to help you in identifying some areas which may be interesting to you. Somehow you must put your list together.

Before making your selection you need to make

the second assessment. Why do you want to do whatever it is you are thinking of doing?

This question will be raised many times in the following pages. It will also be asked by your family and by your neighbors. Your in-laws and even your butcher may ask why you are returning to school. You must have your answers ready. These answers cannot be quick or angry. They must be answers that will convince the questioner of the seriousness of your purpose.

You may have many reasons for doing what you are planning to do. You don't have to explain all of these reasons to anyone but you should be willing to think about them yourself. You must be honest with yourself.

If this return to school is a means of "breaking out" of your present life you will have to look at the specific elements you wish to escape. The housework, unless you can hire help or convince someone to help you, will still be there waiting for you. The family members will also still be there and the relationships may, indeed, feel more tension than before.

Although returning to school cannot be viewed as an escape, your life will be different and, more important, you will be different. For some, the amount of difference will be slight, for others it will be enormous. A desire for this difference may be the real reason you are returning to school and it can be a positive part of your relationship with your family and family life-style.

Planning A Career

Once you have identified your full reasons for returning to school and have identified the final goals you want to reach, which may include preparations for a new career, you can begin to make some specific plans. Which of the dreams left on your list will fit in best with your true reasons for returning to school?

If you are looking to prepare yourself for a new career, consider the choices on your list. Which career do you think will be the most fulfilling? You may have many criteria on which you will base your judgment. Potential salary and job availability may be more important to some people than to others. The amount of authority, the ability to be creative, the opportunity to work with and assist people, and the almost indefinable "interest" quotient of the job are criteria which others find important. A job which is a dream for one person may be a nightmare for someone else.

If you are career oriented, some very important questions are "Can I get the job I want with the degree I am preparing for?" "Are there jobs in this area?" "Will I have to move in order to get a job?" "If I move to another part of the country will I still be able to get a job in this type of work?" "Will I be happy in this type of work?" This last question is going to require some investigation on your part. What are the day-to-day and even hour-to-hour tasks that a person does in this career choice?

Try to talk with people who are already in the field you are considering entering. This may be difficult in some cases but the result will certainly be worth the effort. If you cannot actually talk to anyone in this profession, guidance counselors in high school or in a college may be able to set up some opportunities for you to meet people who are in your soon-to-be chosen field.

If your major emphasis is on personal development you may have to do some "mental exploring" on your own. What types of personal development will mean the most to you? You and your family will be involved in a certain amount of sacrifice. If you are not preparing for some kind of career which will in some financial sense be a "repaying" of everyone involved, you must find a balance between your personal satisfaction and that of other family members. In some families there is no problem. In others, the potential student will have to be very clear about what she wishes to do before discussing the plans with her family.

Before you finally decide on what you are going to do, go over the catalogues from the schools which may be possible for you to attend. Can you get into the school and the program? What are the prerequisites for your program? Can you meet them? There is, for example, little hope of getting into medical school if you have dropped out of the college track some time ago. The same is not true of law or of business. In these areas, experience is valued. Are there special tests you must pass for admission? This is something you must determine well in advance of entrance. A year in advance is not too long in some cases.

Assessing Yourself

Again and again the question returns, "What do you really want?" If you are having difficulty drawing up your list, perhaps the following approach can get you started. Journalists use the who, when, where, how and why technique when they are writing a news story. Use this same technique on yourself. Some of these questions may help you.

Who are you? What kind of personality do you have? Are you quiet? Are you outgoing? Do you want to change or are you happy this way? Does the career you are considering fit with your personality? What are you like physically? Does the new career fit with your physical abilities? You may have eliminated a career such as "tightrope walker" as not being within your physical abilities but have you considered the physical demands of the career of your choice? Will you have to stand for long periods of time, for example, or will you have to do work which demands very good eyesight?

What courses have you taken in school before? What courses did you like? What jobs or volunteer activities have you held? What did you like about them? What didn't you like about them?

When will you like to work? Do you enjoy working on a schedule or do you like to make your own time? Are you a nine-to-five person? Do you want to work all year or do you want to do seasonal work? In some job areas this is possible.

Where do you want to work? Do you want to work with people or do you want to work where you will have to concentrate on the task. Do you want to work indoors or outdoors, in the same location every day or do you want to move around?

How can you do the job? Do you have the attributes associated with this job? Do you have the basic skills? Will a little training prepare you or do you need a lot of training?

Why do you want to select an area of work? Why are you going back to school? We return again to the same question.

chapter **3**

How to Understand Your Feelings About Going Back to School

Many cultures use masks to represent emotions in their dramatic presentations. The old Chinese and Japanese plays have elaborate masks which are immediately recognized by the audience. The Greek masks representing comedy and tragedy often appear in theater programs. In the twentieth century we seem to use an expressionless personal mask to hide our emotions rather than display them. In the days when I rode the New York City subway system, I often wondered how we could all stand and sit so intimately and remain so consistently without expression. For us, it was a means of survival. Unfortunately, many people must hide their feelings even from themselves as a means of personal survival. The woman returning to school may find herself struggling with a number of different feelings.

17

We are all aware of some of our feelings but there are feelings we may be hiding even from ourselves. As women, whether we consider ourselves to be at the "liberated" or at the "nonliberated" end of the scale, we have been subject to a number of cultural pressures which result in a multiplicity of feelings and emotions.

The impact of cultural concepts on our own self-perception is tremendous. What does it mean to each of us to be a woman? As children we first discovered, in our own homes, what it meant to be a woman. Consciously or unconsciously we developed a mental model of what it meant to be a woman and a standard against which we measure our successes and failures. This model may closely resemble our mother or other women in our lives, or it may be related to an image of what a mother should be. Whether we are aware of it or not, we measure ourselves against this model of woman with which we identified as a child. For many the word "woman" is synonymous with the word "mother." Many of the emotional stresses faced by women today are the result of their being unable to separate these two words.

I am not losing sight of the fact that many women are not mothers. They do not have to solve the problems of role separation faced by the woman who is wife, mother, student and sometimes employee. They are often faced, instead, with a conscious or subconscious sense of failure as a woman because they are not mothers. Although this pattern is gradually changing, the women we are discussing here grew up when this was the culturally accepted pattern. They, too, must learn to think of themselves in positive terms.

Although the emotional needs of women returning to school may differ in specifics, they fall, in general, into the same kinds of problems. Concerns about family care, about selecting a program in a particular school, and lack of confidence in doing the work can be handled for the most part by planning and preparation. Other problems which may stem from the struggle to be an individual—the fear of selfishness and the jealousy of spouse, family or friends are not worked out so systematically. The resulting emotional problems may never be really resolved, just handled in a day-to-day fashion. For some it will be a matter of becoming secure with one's own identity. If you are to be really important to others you must begin by developing a positive self image.

The woman returning to school must separate her concepts of the role of woman and the role of mother and wife. There are some very real concerns about family physical needs which must be faced. (They are discussed elsewhere in the book.) Psychological needs must also be met by everyone. There is the question of whether you as a woman can take the time, the money, and the energy to fulfill your needs. Do you have any right to even identify your needs until everyone else's needs have been met? For some the answer will be a clear "yes." Others who would respond in the same way may realize that they have not been acting as if this were so. They feel guilty because they have been thinking about themselves.

Fear of Being Selfish

The fear of being selfish categorizes the feelings of many American women. This does not mean that a great deal of time, energy and money are not spent by the American woman and for the American woman. It means that there are certain ways in which it can be spent which are considered "selfish" by the culture, and other ways are considered "o.k." For example, it is "o.k." to spend two hours on the phone every day with friends or walking through the department stores and malls but it would be selfish to spend two hours per day taking a course at a college. It is "o.k." to spend $15 to $20 having your hair done but it is extravagant—selfish—to spend the same amount on a book you want to read or on a textbook. When I present these examples you see the point immediately, yet how often have you felt selfish for those very reasons. You, as a woman returning to school, must consider how much you are influenced by this fear of being selfish. How often has it held you back? How much of it can you dispel by consciously recognizing this fear and rethinking a number of things?

First of all let us consider the people in your life against whom you may be displaying "selfishness." What is your relationship with your husband, if he is on this list? What is your husband like? Is he a secure or insecure person? Does he share his ideas and his problems with you or are you like a wife in a television commercial? If he is a sharing person, you will be able to share your ideas and dreams with him, convincing him that your going back to school will be good for both of you and good for the family. If he is jealous, if he feels that your progress will somehow take something away from him, you will have to realize that the selfishness is with him and not with you. This may help you to make the internal adjustment to do it anyway.

It has often been said that in every marriage

there are two marriages. Each partner has a different view of the reality of the marriage. A number of studies have been carried out to identify what each "side" in the marriage thinks about the other. In many cases the other pasture is always greener, and more fun. Traditionally men reported feeling that their wives had much more freedom in structuring their time while their wives felt that the men's day was exciting. With more and more women working so that the family can survive economically few women have this freedom any more. Women in the same study indicated that they wanted to be more than wives. They wanted to be more self-sufficient but they felt their men did not want this. The men, in the same study, reported that they wanted their women to be more self-sufficient.

Do not let what you believe to be your husband's resistance to your plan stop you. He may not be resistant to the idea of your going back to school, he may only be resistant to the details of the return. You have a right, as a human being, to think of yourself, to a degree. Do not let anyone call you selfish because you want to go back to school. You cannot postpone such a return indefinitely. You cannot wait always at the end of the line. Take your chance now, get over your fear of being selfish.

CHILD CARE

The greatest emotional traumas may come for the woman with small children. Yes, your children need you, but a number of studies indicate that they do not need you all of the time. Studies made on the children of working women indicate a number of positive qualities in relation to returning to school.

Over and over it has been demonstrated that the quality of the time spent with children is more important than the quantity of time. In evaluating the emotional health of children entering school or in lower grades in school, a number of studies have indicated that the best situation may be either a working or a nonworking mother who is happy doing what she is doing. The nonworking mother who does not want to be home is the worst situation in these tests.

In a study summarized in McCall's July 1979 issue, the self image of daughters was shown to be directly related to the self image of their mothers. Daughters had a good self image if their mothers had a good self image and were doing what they wanted to do whether it was staying at home or working. If you are worrying about the effect your return to school may have on your children, remember that you can make it a positive one for them. Many studies have shown that the educational level reached by the mother has a profound influence on the child. Child care is important and this will be discussed later. Remember to give your children, as well as your husband, some special time to be with you. Remember to think of everyone, including yourself.

There are some very real, physical questions which must be resolved in relation to what will happen to your children that could form the basis for a set of emotional conflicts.

Child care is a very important question to be solved, but there are many solutions. Involve your husband if you can. You may exchange services with another student, or find someone who will care for your children after school. You may get help from a member of your family or you may have to choose a child care center. If you are forced to follow the latter route choose the center very carefully.

Child Care Centers

Make up a very detailed checklist for yourself. Do not think that because a center is licensed it is adequate. It may not even be clean! There is a tremendous difference in such centers. The community agencies which have jurisdiction over child care centers do not usually have sufficient personnel or legal support to actually control the centers. Our local newspaper has started to publish the names and the reason for failure of those which receive a citation or have not passed an inspection. Check the centers that receive a number of citations right off your lists.

Check on the number of people who are supervising the children at any one time. Could you take care of fifteen or twenty two-year-olds alone? The thought may stun you as it did me, yet this happens in many centers. Where do the children nap? How clean is it? Are the mats washed after use or does each child have its own mat? How safe is the playground? What if someone gets hurt? Does anyone know first aid? Check the credentials of all of the people caring for your children, not just the owner of the center. What are the ages of children who are put together? How far is the center from your projected school? Could you stop by between classes to visit with your children? What kind of food is served? How clean is it?

Play is an important activity for little children but it should have some structure part of the time. Developmental aspects should be considered when children's activities are planned. Do your children like the center?

I have only included a few of the points which should go into your checklist for final consideration about selecting a day care center. There are a number of excellent books and magazine articles written about day care center selection. Use these to develop a checklist.

Relationship With Older Children

If you have older children, stop and think about what those children are like. How are you important to them? Will your role be changing with respect to them? Will they be going away to school or moving out on their own? Has your role already changed without you even realizing it? If you assume a new role, how will it really affect them? Remember to think of yourself as a person, not just as the washer of clothes and the cooker of food. I do not mean to minimize these roles, but remember that as your children get older they respond to you more as a person than they do to you as a fulfiller of physical needs. Enriching yourself may increase your closeness with your family. Most children will really understand your need to be a person, your need for enrichment. Do not be afraid of returning to school because of fear of emotional conflicts with your children. Be sure to talk with them about it, and be sure to make time for the things that are really important to them. Remember that after they leave home you will still have yourself and your needs to deal with. You don't have to wait until then to do something about yourself.

One emotion you may have to face is hardly ever

classified as an emotion, and yet it has kept many women from doing things which would be meaningful to them—the fear of being silly.

FEAR OF RIDICULE

Ridicule is a very effective weapon, especially when wielded by your "best" friend. Indicating how silly it is at your age to return to school and regaling the bridge club with her comments may not really be an attempt to hurt you. It may be done from jealousy or ignorance. It may be the result of an excess of cultural pressure. Ignore it. You are more important than your friend's idea of what you should be. If you want to do something more, go and do it. There may be many, including your vocal friend (or family member), who really wish they had the courage and ability to do what you are doing but they are afraid to admit it.

Try not to open yourself up to ridicule by these people. Don't suddenly start dressing like a teenager. Don't bring up the discussion of school if you know how they will react. You may need to have a private talk with your so-called friend. Your husband, who may be getting some of the ridicule also, may have to make a few points with any male friend or relative who is ridiculing your going back to school.

Remember to replace their ridicule with your sense of pride in what you are doing. When a young person goes off to college, he/she opens up a new world for him/herself, making a new circle of friends in the process. A woman returning to school will also make new friends but she will have to retain some of the old relationships as well. When it comes to family, in particular, relationships will have to be kept. If people are insulting you, making fun of you, manage not to be around them. Avoid them. Be secure in what you are doing.

FEAR OF FAILURE

The fear of failure is one of the strongest emotions that must be handled by the woman returning to school. While emotional conflicts often involve other people, the fear of failure involves the sense of your own ability. The fear may not be imagined. You have no way to judge until you actually try whether or not you can actually do the work. It is difficult to assess your own ability. You are probably aware that many people do fail. Remember that many people succeed as well. You have to set your goals at a reasonable level.

Did you try to go to school before? Did you graduate from college? What happened when you went to school? Could you do the work? Why not? Was it a matter of motivation, maturity or background skills? What has happened over the years to change your attitudes? What has happened to your skills? It is quite possible that your attitudes have become very positive but that your skills have become very rusty.

The fear of failure is an emotion which must not be overlooked or ignored. If you are lacking confidence, do some things to actually evaluate your ability. Get some of the books which were written to prepare you for "college boards" or graduate record exams. Try the tests that are included. Can you answer the questions? How are your basic skills? Use Part 2 of this book to evaluate your skills. Make some real and realistic judgments about your abilities.

After you have made these judgments, try to select classes that you can handle. Don't do too much at one time but, on the other hand, don't minimize your ability. Think positively about yourself.

Think positively but think realistically. Have you failed before? Have you had problems going to school before? What were the causes of your problems? How can you eliminate those causes from your present plan? Remember that you are older than you were the last time you went to school. In some ways this is good. Hopefully you have matured and are bringing increased motivation to your plan for returning to school. On the other hand, because you are older, your physical reflexes, even the speed with which your eyes can move, may have slowed. You may also be out of step with learning if it has been a long time since you were in school.

Do not be discouraged if you do not feel completely comfortable about returning to school. Do not let your very natural fears keep you from returning. If you think about the amount of stress, the number of emotions you will be feeling, you may panic. You may have a right to panic, but don't. Take one thing at a time. Think of how you can minimize stress. Plan all the things that can be planned and think about the most important emotions of all—the excitement you will experience when adding a new dimension to your life and the pride you will have in your successes.

chapter 4

How to Get Your Family to Be on Your Side

The members of your family, and in some cases you must include friends, are an important part of your life. Remember that you are an important part of their lives also. If you are going to change your life by going to school, you are going to change their lives also. Your going to school will have both psychological and physical effects on your family. They may react in many different ways. They may not react at all at first but experience a time delay in their reaction.

If you can get your family to be on your side, you will be greatly helped in your return to school. It is certainly not impossible to do, in spite of their feelings, but it will be more difficult if you do not get their cooperation.

What does it mean to have your family on your side? It means that they agree with what you are doing. It means they understand what you are doing. It means they will help you in many ways. They may sacrifice some money so you can go back to school. They may take over some chores that you now do. They may give you some of the privacy you will need to study and work. It means that they are happy if you are happy. It does not mean that they will sing while they do the dishes you used to do. It does not mean that they will never complain. It does not mean that they don't love you if they complain. You love your family and you complain, if only to yourself, about the tasks that are necessary to maintain your home. You don't "not love" your family if you don't "love" to clean a dirty oven. Don't think they don't love you if they are not anxious to take on some of the tasks that you have been doing.

What you are trying to obtain is help over the "long haul." Help them to understand so they will help you. How do you get them to understand? Once more we go back to the question of why you are returning to school. You know the reasons. How do these reasons relate to your family? If you have some negative feelings toward your family and the desire to return to school stems in part from these negative feelings, don't let your family know them if you want their help. It will be best for you if your wish to continue your education is derived from positive feelings.

If your return to school will prepare you for a career earning a better salary then you are now able or equipped to earn, this might be a positive point with your family. If money is a negative factor, as in the case of a husband who says he makes enough money to support his family, don't mention money at all. Speak of your personal development. Try to make them understand that you want to follow some interests. As they have friends and interests, a job, perhaps a profession, you also want to have interests. Returning to school will provide an opportunity for you for personal development.

Getting Your Family's Support

There are several family units you must deal with. In many instances the primary person whose assistance and "blessing" you will need is your husband. If the person reading this is divorced, widowed, never married, separated, or so alienated that no amount of discussion would produce a positive attitude on the part of the husband, you will have to work with the next round which is generally the children. After that, or in some cases before you approach the children, you may have to deal with other relatives, parents, in-laws, brothers and sisters, or friends.

The first thing to do before you speak to any of these groups is to have a very good idea of what it is you want to do and why you want to do it. If there is some member of your family whom you feel would be extremely supportive and give you many good ideas, you might consider talking with them, but in general you should work out your plan yourself. You are not looking for a solution to someone else's life. You are looking for creative answers to your own life. You must be secure in what you want to do and why before you are called upon to defend yourself. You may be very surprised at the number of people who will consider what you are doing as silly, a waste of money and/or time. If you are going to be able to answer these people—and if you live with them you will have to provide some answers—you must have answered these same questions to your own satisfaction. You must have some reasons to believe that what you are doing will be good for you and be able to defend them. You may have reasons that you don't want to reveal and there is no necessity to do so. First you must convince yourself.

SAVING TIME

If your family is close and fairly open to discussion, make them feel involved in your plans. If you have teenage children, you may be surprised at what they know about local schools. If you are already working, they may be used to having you divide your time and attention between them and a job. If you are going to continue to work, you will further encroach on the time you spend together. Assure them you are aware of this and will plan some special time together to make up for it. As you want your family to look at you as an individual, look at each of them as individuals. What do you think they will say when you tell them? What do you think they will be most worried about? Plan some words of reassurance for them. Let them know you have considered them, that you will consider their needs. Above all, however, be firm. Consider yourself, be sure.

If you are going to have time to do studying and attend classes in addition to what you are now doing, you are going to have to find help. Most people are not able to hire outside help and will have to call on some other members of the family. What are some of the jobs that take up the most time? What are some of the jobs that only you can do? Are you sure that only you can do them? It may be the time for your daughter or son or husband to learn to do the shopping or fix a dinner. It may be time to cut down on the chauffeuring that you have been doing. People will depend on you to do things as long as you keep doing them. Can you work out carpooling arrangements with other parents? This may be something that you have avoided doing until now.

Make a list of the categories of things you do. Some of these things are very important to you and to your family, others are less important. Working mothers have long discovered that it is not the quantity of time you spend with your children but the quality of time that is important. Do you shop several times a week or do you do only one large shopping? Your family cares about what is bought, not how many trips you make to the store. Do you do fancy cooking or plain cooking? Sometimes so called "plain cooking" takes more time and clean-up effort. Think about working out a series of recipes that will satisfy the taste desires of your family and yet give you the time to do what you want to do. Have some emergency dinners in the freezer or the "makings" in the cabinet or refrigerator for those days when nothing goes right and you are running late.

In some families you may be able to get help in the shopping or cooking line but this may not be possible in all. One thing that can be done in every family is help with the clean-up after dinner. Except for small children, everyone can bring their dishes to the sink and rinse them off. If you have a dishwasher they can then put them in the dishwasher. If not, they can take a turn with the dishes. If everyone helps, this daily chore can go quickly. One very important thing to remember—so important that it is almost a motto—"Nobody eats off the floor, anyway."

You can only do so many things. You will have to decide just where the line will have to be drawn between sanitary and "able to eat off the floor." The time you are spending scrubbing is not really time spent with your family.

Changing Habits

Another thing that is costly in both time and money is running errands in the car all the time. Are you in a habit of driving unnecessarily? In many cases children can walk to the places that they are used to being driven. This is not true in all cases, and questions of safety must be faced, but ask yourself if you are not making many unnecessary trips.

Another secret "time-waster" is talking on the telephone. This too is a habit for some, almost a secret habit. If you are going to add other dimensions to your life, you may have to eliminate some of the activities you used to pursue. Friends may be reluctant to release you from some of your old commitments such as long phone calls. You will have to let them know you would love to be able to spend the time but you have to cut down. If you are going to ask your family to pitch in, you will have to do some rearranging of your life too. What you must aim for is a rearrangement of time so that the family's emotional and psychological needs are met. After that comes hunger and clean but remember that no matter what you do, no one is going to eat off the floor!

chapter 5

How to Choose a College

To an outsider all colleges and universities may seem to be alike. In reality, they are very different. In order for you to be able to choose a college, you must begin by creating a "report card" for each of the institutions you are considering.

EVALUATING SCHOOLS

Location may be one of your most important criteria. Are there any colleges near you? How far would you be able to travel? Is there public transportation or do you have your own transportation? How expensive will it be to travel to the school? The real cost in both time and money for travel will depend on how many trips to the college you will have to make for each course. Does a college with a main campus that is too far for you to travel to offer classes at an off-campus site? Many colleges offer some classes at sites in local high schools, for example. Don't assume that they don't. Call and check.

Have you considered moving? This may seem to be an extreme solution but you should consider it. For some families it may be impossible but for others it should at least be considered. Somehow one assumes that every woman is married with a husband and a young family. This is not true in many cases. Some women are widowed, divorced, separated, or never married. A move may be temporary, for the duration of a college program. The move itself may open up new opportunities for the individual.

Accredited Schools

All colleges and universities are not of the same quality. In order to protect students and to police their own members, colleges and universities have formed organizations to accredit the institutions. If you are going to attend a college, be certain that it has been ACCREDITED by one of the major accrediting agencies. The six major accrediting agencies and the states they cover are:

Middle States Association of Colleges and Secondary Schools: Delaware, District of Columbia, Maryland, New Jersey, New York, Pennsylvania, Canal Zone, Puerto Rico, Virgin Islands.

New England Association of Schools and Colleges: Connecticut, Maine, Massachusetts, New Hampshire, Rhode Island, Vermont.

North Central Association of Colleges and Secondary Schools: Arizona, Arkansas, Colorado, Illinois, Indiana, Iowa, Kansas, Michigan, Minnesota, Missouri, Nebraska, New Mexico, North Dakota, Ohio, Oklahoma, South Dakota, West Virginia, Wisconsin, Wyoming.

Northwest Association of Secondary and Higher Schools: Alaska, Idaho, Montana, Nevada, Oregon, Utah, Washington.

Southern Association of Colleges and Schools: Alabama, Florida, Georgia, Kentucky, Louisiana, Mississippi, North Carolina, South Carolina, Tennessee, Texas, Virginia.

Western Association of Colleges and Schools: California and Hawaii.

If the college you attend is not accredited, you may find that your degree is not worth anything. It may not be accepted to get a job or a license. Credits taken at an institution that is not accredited will not usually be accepted at an accredited institution. If the college you are thinking of attending is accredited, they will publish that in their catalogue. If you have any doubts, write to the association that covers the area in which the school is located. They will tell you if the school is accredited and if the program in which you are interested is accredited.

In addition to the accrediting associations, some majors which require licensing may have to be approved by other groups such as state agencies and professional organizations. Courses to be used to obtain a teaching license, medical and law programs fall into this classification.

How can you find out if the school you are considering has the proper accreditation? You might begin by asking the appropriate person in the school.

The appropriate person is not a secretary or even a counselor. It is the registrar or the admissions director or the head of the program in which you are interested. If you are unsure of the reputation of the school, write to the regional association. You may also want to ask at another school in the neighborhood. I am quite aware of the programs and the accreditation of the other universities in the geographic area and have often answered questions for students who are trying to decide among programs. I know that I try to give a fair description and I believe that most program directors do the same. It is not a good thing, but some nonaccredited schools try to convince students that it doesn't matter whether a school is accredited or not. Don't believe them. I have tried to comfort many students who took courses in nonaccredited colleges, even finished their degrees, and found they had to start over. Some schools are in the process of getting accredited. This also has proved to be a problem for students because some of those schools pass the accreditation process and some fail it. Don't take chances. You do not have the time or money.

Programs

After you have found a school or a number of schools that fit your location criterion and are accredited, you have to take a look at their programs. It seems like the catalogue is always "out of print" or at the printers. This is a fact of life I have discovered over the years. If you write or call a college, the college catalogue will be sent to you if it is available. That last phrase is the key. Catalogues now cost at least two dollars and often more to print; mail costs increase the burden on the admissions department of the college. There are a limited number of catalogues printed and when they are gone the incoming student must wait until a new catalogue is available. Some colleges charge for their catalogues. It is best to visit the campus and get a feeling for the place. What is it like? If there are no catalogues available, you will still be able to look at one.

Select the program or programs in which you might be interested and make an appointment to talk with a counselor or professor in that area. What would you have to take? How long would it take you? What are the students like who take that program? What can you do with that degree? Are you prepared to enter that program? Will you have to take entrance examinations? When are they given? How competitive is the program? Would you be able to get in?

All of life is a gamble. You must decide just what chances you want to take. I can tell you what to ask but I cannot tell you just what decisions you should make on the basis of the answers you receive. They will depend on your ability and your own perception of self. I am by nature a fairly conservative person, I suppose, but I would recommend that unless you are fulfilling a lifelong ambition, you choose a program that will allow you to select options partway through. Most programs have a basic curriculum for the first two years. You must be sure that you are taking the correct courses, however.

Will you be able to do the coursework? If you have never been able to do addition, should you choose a program that requires several courses in statistics? The decision is yours. Remember, however, that you really do want to succeed. You may be interested in taking some special courses or you may be interested in taking a complete degree program. The scope of your decisions will be very different. Beginning with a single course will allow you to test your ability to do college level or graduate level work. If you are planning on completing a degree, you probably do not want to waste any time or money. If you select a course which could be used to meet the requirements of one or more of the different courses of study you are considering, you can accomplish two things. You will meet a requirement for an anticipated degree and you will test yourself and the program by taking a single course.

There are many different kinds of degrees. The Associate of Arts (A.A.) and the Associate of Science (A.S.) are given by community or junior colleges after two years of study. The Bachelor of Arts degree and the Bachelor of Science degree are received after a traditional four year program. It may take you more or less time to actually finish the degree depending on your background, course of study, and rate of study. The Masters of Arts degree and the Masters of Science degree are traditionally given after one or two years of full-time study. This degree is often completed on a part-time basis by people already working in a particular field such as teaching. There are many variations on the Master's degree, specialized for certain professions. If you are considering a program which offers a specialized degree such as a Masters in Public Administration, be certain that that degree will be accepted by the profession and any accreditating association which may be involved. Check these yourself.

The doctoral degree represents a number of years of study beyond the bachelor's degree. The same comment about variations in the degree title made with respect to the masters applies to the doctorate.

ADMISSION POLICIES

Admission policies vary from school to school. Some schools have very high acceptance standards and require that you take a specific entrance test. Some schools are very competitive and you must apply almost a year in advance. If you are trying to get into such a school, you should apply to other schools as "backup" in case you don't get into the one of your choice. To optimize your chance, study for the tests that are given and take great care in filling out the application form and in answering any questions you may have to prepare.

The organizations that prepare the tests say that studying doesn't help. Don't believe them. There are many ways in which studying helps. (Read the section on test-taking in this book for some additional ideas for preparing to take tests). The tests are, in many cases, based on what is supposed to be general knowledge and were originally prepared for students who are just getting out of high school. These students are used to taking exams; they have just learned the work which is included and many of them study very hard for the tests. There are preparatory books for studying for these exams. Get them at your bookstore. Don't settle for the little pamphlets sent to you by the group which makes up the tests. You will need to improve your vocabulary and your comprehension skills. There may be logic and math problems which you haven't done in years. Put yourself on a real study schedule and prepare yourself to do well on these exams. Remember if you don't do well you will have to wait quite a period of time before you can retake them.

Entrance Exams

One of the exams is the Scholastic Aptitude Test (SAT) prepared by Educational Testing Service, Princeton, N.J. The aptitude tests and the more specific achievement tests are often called "college boards." They are given six times a year on Saturdays and are taken by millions of students every year. Since they are given only on specific dates and a certain amount of time is needed for them to report your grade, you must plan ahead to take the test by the right date for entrance to specific schools.

This statement is also true for the Graduate Exam (GRE) required by many graduate schools, the Law School Admission Test (LSAT) for students who desire to go to law school, and the Admission Test for Graduate Study in Business (ATGSB). Each of these exams is administered by the Educational Testing Service in Princeton, N.J. Foreign students may be required to take the Test of English as a Foreign Language (TOEFL) which demonstrates their proficiency in English. Information on this exam may be obtained from TOEFL, Box 899, Princeton, New Jersey 08540.

Students who desire admission to medical schools or dental schools will have to take specific exams such as Medical College Admission Test (MCAT) or Dental Admission Test (DAT). Specific testing details may be obtained from the school to which you are applying.

There is no such thing as a passing grade on

any of these exams. Each school sets its own standard as to what score they will consider acceptable as a lower limit. If you have a score higher than this limit you are not admitted automatically. You will then be considered by the admission committee on the basis of other criteria. There have been a number of court cases recently (including the Bakke case in California) regarding schools which have different admission criteria for different groups. If you are not admitted to a school, find out why. There may have been an error or you may not be qualified. In either case it is important to understand why you were not admitted.

I know of cases in which the inquiry resulted in a review of the application and the students were eventually admitted. I also know of cases in which the students came to realize that they just did not have the background nor were they able to demonstrate the ability required in a particular school and saved themselves frustration and failure by applying to another area of study or to another school.

There are a number of schools which have a policy known as "Open Admission." This practice may appear under a number of different titles but basically it means that the student is not required to pass any admission tests. He or she may only be required to have a high school diploma for college entrance or a college diploma (from an accredited school) for graduate school admission. If you are not able to plan far enough ahead to go through a complicated admission process which includes national tests, you might consider taking courses in such a school or program. Make sure that these courses are regular college courses and can be transferred to another school. Usually you are required to maintain a certain grade standard to remain in such a program, but it does offer a good opportunity to the older person who is returning to school. You may do well in courses but not have the skills or confidence to do well on the national test.

Applications

One thing you will find when filling out applications and other forms is that they were designed for young people who are coming out of high school. In spite of the fact that large numbers of people are going to school from every age group, even the government and bank loan applications assume you are eighteen years old and supported by your parents. Do not be discouraged by the forms. Fill in what is applicable. Most of us have no idea what our parents' social security numbers are since our parents have not supported us for many years. There are many examples which seem humorous when repeated but were a source of frustration to the woman involved. In some cases the woman was supporting the parents but that was difficult to get into those little boxes which are designed for computer input. If you have been living on your own or have your own family and have not received support from your family for a number of years, do not be forced into listing your parents' income on the form. Put a statement like Not Applicable, Adult, Live with Husband and Children—whatever applies. The computer may reject your application but you will be able to get a personal hearing. Be sure you can document (income tax returns, separate address, etc.) that you do not live with nor are supported by your parents.

One term you may need to understand when you are comparing colleges is type of credit you will receive for a course. A course you take has a certain credit "value." You do not get a degree based on the number of courses you take but on the number of credits you earn. There are two basic kinds of credit values, although with the flexibility in schools today there may be other variations. One type of credit is called semester hours and the other is called quarter hours. The word credit may be substituted for the word hours. Some schools divide their school year into a fifteen-week block of time called a semester while others use a nine- or ten-week block known as a quarter. A course earning one semester credit meets for sixteen hours while a course earning a quarter credit meets for nine hours. An exchange system is set up so that one quarter credit equals two-thirds of a semester credit. For example, nine quarter hours are the equivalent of six semester hours. This distinction is important when comparing costs, length of program, and ability to transfer.

A number of colleges and universities have been experimenting with varied formats. Some of these formats involve the use of instructional systems such as television, preprogrammed materials and computer-assisted instruction. Some programs are ideal for the woman returning to school and some are not.

If you are having difficulty arranging a schedule which allows you to attend classes on campus, a course over television may be ideal for you. On the other hand, if you are returning to school to help develop yourself as a person, such a course will lack the interpersonal involvement you need. You must also be certain that the credits you earn, both in the programs listed above and in programs which have accelerated formats or limited contact hours, are accepted by other programs in the school, by other schools, and by the profession you are attempting to enter.

There are many things which must be considered when you are deciding whether a program will actually meet your needs. Once more you should generate some lists comparing the different programs you are considering. If you develop such maps to your own future, you will not only help yourself make the right choices, you will establish confidence in your decision-making process. You will also be able to explain your decisions more credibly to your family and friends. You will eliminate some of the stress from your decision to return to school. Don't be afraid of making lists. They are not silly and you don't have to show them to anyone!

One very realistic thing to consider from the beginning is planning on attending two schools. There are many reasons that may form the basis for this choice. Cost is one possible reason. You may want to take some of your basic courses in a less expensive school and transfer to another school for the more specialized courses, or you may want to take your basic courses in a larger university and transfer to a smaller, more individualized institution for the specialized program. You may want to begin your work in a place that will give you some individualized attention and then transfer to a larger institution which may have many more offerings when you get to the advanced stages of your work. You may want to travel less during the beginning of your program and agree to a longer trip during the later stages for reasons which are important to you. Only you can make the decision as to what is the best plan for you.

If you are considering combining work at more than one school, one important thing is to determine in advance if the second school will give you full credit for the work you do at the first school. You can ask that a program outline be set up for you which will indicate which courses taken at one school will fulfill your program at another school. Many students, both those who are going to college directly from high school and those who are returning to school, have been disappointed by not having credits transferred. Remember that every program within an institution has its own requirements. Courses taken at a college may not be accepted towards a different program at the same college because of the requirements of that program.

Although, in many cases, a college education is a buyer's market today, colleges and universities are in principle maintaining their standards of education. It may still be difficult to get into the program you desire. You may have to pass general examinations or college examinations in order to have your name placed on an acceptance list. An interview and/or letters of reference may be required. Although your heart may be set on a certain program in a certain school, it is best if you apply to more than one place so that you will have some immediate alternative if you are not accepted in the one of your choice. The program that turned you down may be losing a star pupil but, also, they might have been right.

There are many kinds of schools. There are state

schools, large universities, small universities, and
community colleges. There are some colleges that
are affiliated with certain religious groups and there
are other private institutions, both large and small,
that survive in spite of the fact that they do not receive money from public sources.

If the schools you are considering pass your
other criteria—location, accreditation, cost, programs, and you still have a few names on your list,
you must live in a large urban area. Most people
are not fortunate enough to have one school left. If,
however, you are fortunate and still have some
choices to make, one aspect you might want to consider is where you will be comfortable. This, again,
is something you must decide for yourself. If you
are older, you may or may not feel comfortable being
the only older person in your program. If you have
a stable family relationship and other friends, an
environment in which you have some difficulty in
making friends or feeling a part of the group may
not matter to you. I know many older persons (and
when you are returning to school, twenty-five may
be older!) who have fitted in very well with younger
students. If you do find a program that is designed
for people who are returning to school, you may want
to give it serious consideration. Many schools have
established Women's Centers. Make use of the coun-
seling available at such centers.

One pitfall that a student must be aware of is
the "continuing education" and "noncredit" courses
offered by a university. Just because a college or university offers a course, don't automatically assume
that you will get college credit for it. Some institutions give courses for the interest and development
of their students but do not consider them to be part

of a program and will not accept these courses for the degree you seek. Ask first. Don't be hesitant to ask questions. An old saying is a good one to remember here. It is better to be safe than to be sorry.

Special Credit

Many schools will give you credit toward a degree in different ways. You may be able to get credit for learning you have done over the years by passing exams. The College Level Equivalency Program (CLEP) exams developed by the Educational Testing Service of Princeton, N.J. are one example of such examinations. The Testing Service does not give credit. Some schools will give you credit for the exam, depending on your grade. Different schools set a different score as acceptable. There are other examinations similar to CLEP that are accepted by different institutions. Each school will be able to give you information concerning what is acceptable and what score must be obtained.

Even if you are not able to start school right away, you may want to begin studying and taking the CLEP exams. You should apply to the school of your choice and, as you take and pass the CLEP or other exams, have the reports sent to your school. You may begin your studies with a full year or so of work credited to you without ever having been inside a classroom.

Another opportunity for advanced placement comes with what is sometimes called "life experience credit." Some institutions are giving credit for portfolios of work which represent some of the activities you have been carrying on during your nonacademic years. Not all institutions give such credit and each will have their own criteria and requirements for documentation, but you should be aware that this is an opportunity offered by many schools.

Some institutions put a time limit on the credits they will transfer. If you took courses in college a number of years ago, you may or may not be able to transfer them because of their age.

Before you select a college, you must look at a number of factors:

> The quality of the college only measured in part by the accreditation
> The program offerings
> The location
> The cost
> The time at which the courses are offered
> The atmosphere of the institution
> The amount of advanced standing you can obtain

All of these factors must go into your report card on the college. Some of these may be more important to you than others. Accreditation is the only one I want you not to forget.

Get busy and do your report card on the different schools you are considering. You will be surprised to find the new programs and opportunities that schools are offering. You will also be surprised how you have changed over the years.

chapter **6**

How to Find the Money to Go Back to School

COUNTING THE COST

Whoever said that the best things in life were free was never faced with having to pay college tuition bills. College tuition costs, especially in the private sector, have risen dramatically in the past few years. In spite of the increases, student tuitions only pay about 35 per cent of the cost of education in private institutions and an even smaller percentage in public institutions.

Money is not the only cost to be considered when determining the actual cost of your education. There are a number of things you must evaluate. For example, the cost in time, emotional cost, and physical cost may be more "expensive" to you than the actual amount of money you must spend.

In purely financial terms, a college degree is a

good investment. If you are going to make the best
investment you will have to look at a number of factors, only one of which is money. Before you can
finally select a school or estimate just how much
you will have to spend, you will have to think about
each of these things. Make a chart which will show
the following information for the schools you are
considering.

Financial Cost

When estimating the cost of your education, do it
on a course basis and on a total program basis. Are
the courses given for semester credit or quarter
credit? How many credits will you need for your degree? Will the school give you advanced standing
for CLEP or life experience credit? Will the program
in which you are interested transfer courses you
have taken at another institution? Will the program
accept courses taken for another program at the
same university? Do not think that any courses you
take at an institution will be acceptable toward all
programs at that same institution. Every program
has its own requirements and some have special admission requirements that are in addition to the general institutional requirements.

All of these factors will reduce the cost of the
degree. Are you charged on a course-by-course basis
or is it a flat fee for a full-time program? Can you
take advantage of the rate for attending full-time
or will it put too much pressure on you? Are there
registration fees? How much are they and how often
do you have to pay them? If you drop out of a course
will any of your tuition be refunded? How much?
Learn the rules.

There are many forms of financial aid available today which did not exist a few years ago. Recent changes in legislation have expanded some programs so that they will better meet the needs of middle income families and of older students returning to school. Because of the ever-changing set of rules that are associated with most programs, specific information will not be given here. Instead, general information about programs will be given and recommendations for further sources of information will be made.

One important thing to remember if you are trying to obtain financial aid to return to school is that you are not a beggar. You are an individual seeking to do something which may in turn benefit the community itself. As an individual you have a right to look at those sources of funding and seek funding for yourself. As a member of a family, you almost have an obligation to seek some outside funds unless your income level is such that the additional cost of your education will not be a noticeable factor. Don't ever be ashamed of looking for financial aid. The first place to start is at the institutions you are considering attending. Almost every institution has some financial aid available and every one will have some individual designated to give financial aid information.

When should you investigate financial aid? If you have even the slightest glimmer of a thought of returning to school, you should look into your eligibility for financial aid. Some programs have application dates that are many months ahead of the date at which the money would be available to you. If

you miss that date you might have to wait a year
to apply. Other programs may require certain tests
like the college boards and the graduate record exam
which have to be taken on certain dates.

One thing to remember is that you are never
too old to get a scholarship, a loan, a grant or be
part of a work-study program. These topics need to
be reviewed separately. There are differences between these programs, the major one being the matter of having to repay the money.

Scholarships and Grants

Scholarships and grants do not have to be paid back,
although there are conditions for retaining them.
There are scholarships available from a number of
sources.

1. The school itself. Many institutions have scholarships available for students. The award may be
based on academic merit, on need, or on a combination of these qualities. Organizations may have given
money to the school which is to be awarded to someone who wants to study in a particular area. The
school's financial aid office will be able to give you
information.

2. Organizations. There are many organizations
and foundations which provide assistance to students.
Womens' clubs and church groups are sometimes
sources of funds for local colleges.

Foundations established by wealthy families,
sometimes in memory of a deceased member of the
family or as the recipient of a bequest, often have
scholarships available. There are many very small

scholarships and grants that can be obtained in this way. Some are for small amounts, others are full tuition awards. Do not hesitate to apply for small scholarships. They add up.

Some years ago a friend of mine, then in graduate school herself, was faced with the prospect of having to put her youngest brother through college, their father having been dead for many years. She spent some time in the library looking for the names of foundations and scholarship programs. On her search she consulted some books that someone had put together listing different scholarships. Then she searched the newspapers and used the *Reader's Guide to Periodical Literature* to discover magazine articles on scholarship awards and announcements. She contacted local organizations to investigate any scholarships they might have. She did spend some time and money on stamps but she managed to gain several scholarships for her brother ranging from $75 to $350 which covered most of his tuition. Don't be surprised if you do the same thing.

Many programs require a financial aid analysis. Since it is difficult for schools to analyze financial information, many of them make use of an outside agency such as the College Scholarship Service which uses their own financial aid form to perform the analysis.

Grants which also do not have to be paid back are sums of money given by an organization. The government, as well as other organizations, gives grants. Two classifications of grants which the government offers are for undergraduate study only. They are the Basic Educational Opportunity Grants (BEOG), and the Supplemental Educational Opportunity Grants (SEOG). New laws have expanded the income range of eligible students. Because the regulations keep changing, specific requirements will not be listed here. These grants have given many students the opportunity to return to school.

There are many individuals who are still eligible for veteran's benefits. These also have a variety of regulations. Different programs may be approved for different dollar amounts. The Veterans Administration (VA) office can give you guidelines for eligibility.

College work-study programs combine opportunities for work with tuition remission or payment.

3. *Loans.* Loans differ from grants and scholarships in that they must be paid back. Some loans carry reduced interest charges or deferred interest charges and are insured by the government. Federally Insured Student Loans (FISL), and National Direct Student Loans (NDSL) are insured by the government but the loans are arranged with your local bank, and applications are usually secured at the lending institution.

WORK

Work seems to be a four-letter word to some members of the present generation, but to many of us it was the way we obtained what we desired, and when it comes to returning to school it will be the only way we can obtain the money needed for tuition. If you have been working to maintain your family, you may have to consider reducing the number of hours worked if you are going to return to school. You can only do so much, remember. If you have not been working, you may have to find a source of money. If you are returning to school, this is not the time to find a full-time job in addition. Try to find some work which will pay enough for you to meet your additional expenses. The job should make few demands on you, unless it also has a career direction.

Part Time Work

The best thing would be to find a part-time job that is related to your career interests and plans. This might be some kind of an agency job if you are planning on a social-work-related job or as a teaching aide if you are going to be a teacher. If the job is not at all career-related, try to get a job that will not make too many demands on you physically or emotionally. A job as a receptionist or doing some routine work may be satisfactory, and may even give you an opportunity to study. Don't forget that there might be jobs in your neighborhood that could bring in enough money to cover your expenses. Doing errands for others, taking care of children when you have to take care of your own anyway, cooking meals for an elderly person when you have to cook for your own family, typing papers, or doing other "neighborhood" tasks may bring in enough money to cover your additional expenses.

Think of ways to minimize expenses as long as they do not place a drain on you in terms of time. Try forming a car pool with other students to avoid the additional transportation costs. Try swapping babysitting costs with another student (you take mine and I'll take yours). Investigate jobs on campus. You may not be paid as much but you might be able to do them between classes. I used to keep the books for my college's cafeteria and I was able to make my own hours. I found that by getting up early I could work between 6 and 8 A.M. every day and get ten hours of work in every week without interfering with my academic or social life. Many colleges have work-study programs which involve working for your tuition. Some programs are partly federally funded.

Barter

Barter is an old method of paying for things. Are there some talents you have which the college may trade for your tuition? The college may not have thought of the job nor have established a rate for it. There are more opportunities in this area at private schools which are not as bound by regulations as public institutions. Think of the things you can do, think of the things the college may need done. Think of a way in which you can match your abilities with the school's needs. Decide who could make the "deal" and present your plan. Don't be hesitant or embarrassed, be creative. You are trading a talent you possess for a seat in a class. If you don't attend, the college will not get the money for tuition anyway. Let them agree to your presence rather than your absence by performing some task for the college which they, in turn, could not afford to purchase. Be persuasive. Again, remember that you are not a beggar. Don't be ashamed. Barter is the oldest form of trade. Put a good value on your abilities.

While you are planning your finances, remember that tuition is probably going to increase. Colleges face the same increased costs as everyone else and have to raise their rates accordingly. Don't have your costs so tightly planned that you cannot survive a tuition increase.

Remember also that scholarship and grant requirements change from year to year. BEOG regulations have changed this year so that persons with a higher income and home ownership are now eligible. If you are not eligible when you first apply, check eligibility in later years. Rules may change to your benefit.

Whatever you do, keep your head high. Trying to go to school is a good and important thing. Do not be ashamed if you have to do some menial tasks in order to get the money needed. You are planning for a future. Many people who are wealthy today had to work their way through school. Encourage your family to support you. Do not let them be ashamed either. Let them catch enthusiasm from you. They may be more willing to accept small sacrifices they have to make.

Understand that it may be difficult for your husband to see you have to work to put yourself through school. It may not be that he doesn't want you to go to school. It may be that he is ashamed that he doesn't have enough income so that you may do as you wish about returning. It may be that he should have returned himself but did not have the ambition to do so. Be understanding and at the same time be determined. You can do it. Don't let anything stop you.

chapter 7

How to Survive by Planning Your Time or "Nobody Eats Off the Floor Anyway"

Faced with the question of returning to school, many women will say that they only wish they could but they haven't got the time. Oh, if they only had the time! Time, that effervescent quantity that none of us can hang on to. How can you find more time? In order to do that, you must find out where your time is going now.

LISTING ESSENTIALS

I can hear you now saying, "She's going to tell me to take out a piece of paper and make another list!" Yes, I am. No one can write down everything that they do, but try to write down the essentials. In another section we discussed ways to get your family's support; you may be able to get some help with some of the tasks on this list.

I subtitled this chapter with a phrase that I want you to remember. There are things that are essentials and there are things that are habit. These things that are habit are nice to do if you have the time, but everyone will not die of scurvy or bubonic plague if you don't. Put the nicknacks away. You can dust them after you graduate. Keep the family outings. These are important years which you cannot get back. Store-bought cakes and pies taste good, too. Take the time you would have spent in the kitchen and spend it with your family.

Divide your time into three parts, time needed to do the essentials, time needed for self and family, time needed for school.

The time needed to do the essentials should be analyzed so that it is down to an absolute minimum. Try to get all the help you can, try to eliminate extra steps, extra shopping trips, etc. Eliminate all the things that you can eliminate. You have a good excuse for not contributing to every bake sale and every community organization. You will just have to tell your friends that you won't be available for these things for awhile.

Cutting Back Nonessentials

You may have to cut down on some of the things that you used to do for recreation by yourself. Needlework, cards, etc., may have to take a backseat for awhile but keep them available for those times when you just have to take a break. Time spent on exercise and grooming are not wasted minutes. Take care of your health and appearance. You should maintain good eating habits. Don't fall into the "teenage" pattern of a coke and a candy bar for lunch. Keep your weight down. Have a good breakfast. Find a diet that will give you energy and keep you at a good weight. Lose weight if your doctor recommends it. Have some "makings" on hand for a good low calorie, high energy lunch and take it with you. Eating on the run is bad for everyone, but the returning student must be especially careful. Plan your day so that you can have a few minutes for lunch (or dinner depending on your class hours).

Your personal appearance may be more important to your husband and children than you realize. They may feel let down if you start to neglect your appearance. There is a difference between casual and sloppy. Although you may no longer have much time and money available for buying clothes, try to put together enough variations so you don't seem to be wearing the same thing all the time. If you usually have your hair done, continue to have it done whenever possible. You will look better and I find I get a lot of work done under the privacy of the dryer.

The time that you are reserving for family and friends should be well planned. Endless driving around on errands for people is seldom remembered. Make the time count. Make it be special.

MAKING THE MOST OF YOUR TIME

The time that you reserve for school will have to be well planned. You will have certain hours that are set aside for attending class and other hours for outside work. How do you study, how do you handle assignments? Can you get to class an hour early or stay later and spend that time working on assignments? It may be worth the extra effort if it is at all possible so that you can actually get the work done. Trying to combine studying with child care is almost impossible. Your family and friends and you, yourself, will have to understand that you must have some privacy if you are going to get your studying and papers done. Set some specific time aside each day for your work. Set some goals or tasks to be done each day, such as reading 6 pages, working one hour on the paper that is due, etc. Divide up your assignments and the time you have available to do them.

Can you do your tasks in that amount of time? If not, you will have to find more time or improve your skills or both. Look closely at your learning habits so that you may improve them. These will be discussed in detail in a later section.

Every day does not have to be alike. Plan some variety in your days. Perhaps on one day you could do many of your household tasks and on another only school-related work. I know one woman who has five small children, works during the day, and has returned to school to get her college degree. Her plan for survival is such that she devotes herself to her family when she reaches home from work, goes to bed at about the same time as her children and gets up at two o'clock in the morning to do her studying. As she says, she can't work with the children around and she is just too exhausted to do much when they go to bed. Instead of trying to work when she is so tired she gets some rest and finds a few hours when she has some privacy to get things done. I don't think I could get up so early, myself, but the important thing is that she has worked out a plan that works for her. Work out your plan for yourself. Work out your priorities and remember that these may change from one day to another. Establish some pattern that makes sense to you.

chapter 8

You, the Student

There probably exists, somewhere a picture of you starting off to school in a plaid dress, knee socks, sturdy shoes and pigtails. You knew what to wear and your mother knew what you should wear. You knew that you were dressed just right on the first day of school. As a mature student returning to school, you may no longer have confidence that you know just what to wear or how to act with other students and teachers.

CHANGING ROLES

Returning to school is more and must be more than just attending class. A great amount of the learning as well as personal development comes from interaction with fellow students and discussions with teachers. From the beginning you must decide that you will integrate yourself into the group.

How can I, you ask? Those students are the same age as my children! I'd feel silly! First of all you must realize that you are now a person with two roles and two worlds you must meet. As a person in your old role, you have a certain position in your family and in your community. You have a dignity that goes with your years and you have come to expect to be treated according to your position. As a student, even though a mature student, you must remember that you have now taken on a new role. It is a role that is exciting but it is not a role that carries with it a great deal of dignity.

As a student your ideas will have to stand on their own. They will not have merit just because they have been stated by you. Some people, returning to school, have not had their ideas listened to for a long time. They may have fallen into the pattern of doing their daily tasks and not talking about many things that did not fit into the daily schedule. They may have existed in an environment that did not take them into account as a person and as an "idea-maker." These people will have to grow accustomed to phrasing their ideas, to exploring their ideas with others. They will also have to become accustomed to having their fragile, newly-flown ideas attacked by others who don't really mean to hurt them.

Fitting In

Many questions are coming to your mind. How should I dress? How should I act? What should I say?

The answers to these questions will depend on you and on the college you are attending. One of the things you explored when selecting your college was the age and "mix" of the students. If there are a large number of returnees in your classes you will not feel alone. Let us assume that there are not. Because of the limited educational opportunities in your area or because of cost and program, let us assume that you have selected a school that has very few students who are not in the eighteen to twenty-two age range. What do you do?

First of all, and this technique applies to all returning students, thoroughly explore the school you are going to attend before the first day of class or registration. If you are going to feel secure and be comfortable, know the location of everything in the school that you will need to find. Many schools have a map in their catalogue which you can mark and use until you become familiar with the campus layout. These are some of the places you will need to know:

1. Registrar's office or other place of registration.

2. The comptroller's office or the place you will have to pay your tuition and fees.

3. The classrooms. You may be taking classes in many different buildings on campus. It is not always possible to find out in advance where certain classes will meet, but you can be familiar with the names and locations of the different classroom buildings and the way rooms are numbered in these buildings.

4. The bookstore. Many colleges have their own bookstore while others use bookstores located near the school. Besides locating the bookstore, you should explore the possibility of buying your books early.

Sometimes more students sign up for a class than there are books ordered. Books have to be ordered far in advance and, because of the high cost, bookstores are reluctant to "over-order." Do not write in your book when you get it, and keep your receipt. It is possible that you will later decide that you will not take that course or that you have purchased the wrong book or one you will not actually need. Most bookstores will give you credit if you return the book within a specified time after registration and if the book is in "new" condition. This means absolutely perfect condition.

5. *The library.*   Some schools have only one library, other schools have different libraries for different subjects. There may be an education library or a law library or a science library. Find out which libraries contain the material you will need for your work. Explore those libraries. What are the reserve book policies? How does the microfilm reader work? Where are the journals? In general, where are the books you will need located in the library? Don't be ashamed to ask.

6. *The cafeteria and other eating and recreation places.*   Some schools have only one cafeteria and others have more than one. Some schools have additional snack bars. Other schools may depend on a number of local fast food outlets to feed their student body. Some places will allow you to bring your own lunch and eat it in the cafeteria.

Visiting the cafeterias or snack bars will not only give you a chance to find out the procedures, it will give you an opportunity to see what the other students look like. The day students may differ greatly from the evening students. While day students may dress in either a very casual manner or a young fashionable manner, evening students are often coming directly from work and dress as they do for work.

Since you are going to have many new expenses, you will not want to invest money in clothes. If you have been a "housedress" wearer however, you may have to add a few things to your wardrobe. Don't rush into it. Take a look at what is being worn and then adapt it to a style that is comfortable and correct for you.

If everyone is wearing jeans and loose tops and jerseys and you haven't worn them in years, adapt. Wear slacks and tailored shirts or skirts or pantsuits. You can work with fellow students who are much younger than you without taking on all of their customs and clothing choices. A mature person who tries to imitate all of the things her fellow classmates do may end up looking a little silly. If you are comfortable in jeans, wear them if everyone else is wearing them. The important thing is to feel good and right. If your budget is limited, have a few basic slacks or skirts and blouses that can be alternated to give you different looks. No one wears dressy clothes to class. An outfit that would be great for a luncheon meeting will not, in general, be right for college.

Simplicity in hairdo and makeup would also be a good guide. Check out whatever you can check out before classes start.

7. Transportation and parking. Probably one of the most stressful situations for anyone these days is finding a parking place. If you are going to drive to campus, find out the parking regulations. As a visitor investigating the campus, you may have been allowed to park in visitor parking which will be closed to you as a student. If you find that you have to park "miles" from your classes unless you come early, you may have to arrange your schedule differently.

If you are taking public transportation to college, check to see if it really keeps the schedule it publishes. You don't want to constantly be late or even miss class because of a bus or train that isn't dependable.

You will find out all of these things when you start class, you say. Why do you have to check them out ahead of time? The answer is that you want to minimize the stress you will undergo in starting your new venture. The first days of college can be very stressful. The anticipation is great but the reality may be a little bit of a letdown. If you have to run from one line to another, find that the text you needed is sold out, are late for class because you couldn't park and couldn't find the classroom, you will be increasing the burden on your already-taxed self.

Be cool! The phrase goes in and out of popularity but the meaning is very relevant here. The more you can do to keep yourself "cool" during the first days of class, the better able you will be to successfully handle your new role as student.

NEW RELATIONSHIPS

You may be able to help others in finding their way around campus and this may be the beginning of new friendships for you. Very few people find it easy to make friends. I have no problems in getting up to speak before several hundred people but I do find it difficult to add myself to a small group of strangers at a party or meeting. I now believe that almost everyone does. Few people have that blend of pride and self-confidence which enables them to successfully insert themselves into a group of complete strangers who don't know anything about them in advance. Successful politicians who would seem to fit this description, in reality, have advance men and the fact that they are running for office to carry them along. They might be standing with clammy hands on the edges of the crowd if no one knew who they were.

You will have a number of relationships to establish. There are, for example, your role as a member of a class, your relationship with your fellow students as students or as friends, your role if you are interested in dating, and your relationship with your teachers.

Relationship With Teachers

The relationship with your teachers may seem to be inverted to you. Your teacher may be quite a bit younger than you. He or she may remind you of one of your own children, for example. Because of this you may not feel the academic respect that you would have naturally felt if you were young and the teacher were a distinguished professor. As you have had to mentally remove the question of age with respect to your own return to school, so you must remove it with respect to your teachers. Age has no relevance in the classroom. Follow the lead of the other students in their relationship with the faculty. Some people prefer to be addressed on a first name basis, others (the majority) prefer the use of title. Don't be surprised or insulted if you are addressed on a first name basis. This also is the custom. If you are addressed as Mrs. —— when all the other students are called by their first name, you might want to ask (privately) to be called on a first name basis also. This will make you part of the group and make you less "different."

How much should you talk up in class? This is a surprising question perhaps but it is one that reveals one of the largest problems for returning students, the problem of becoming part of the class.

Many women who have spent a number of years at home taking care of house and family are hungry to talk. They have always known that they had something to say, perhaps, but for the most part they were limited to a brief chat with the butcher or a few words with the check-out clerk or a discussion of children or recipes with a neighbor. There was no opportunity for other kinds of discussions. Some returnees are so overwhelmed by the opportunity to express ideas or to ask questions that they never stop. They become a problem in class, both to the professor who does not like to be rude but who has a set of objectives for his or her class and for the other students who came to learn from the teacher and who do not want to listen to someone disrupt their class with continual comments and questions.

I do not want to suggest that the person who is returning to school should not ask questions or participate in class discussion. What I am suggesting is that they monitor themselves closely. Ask yourself, Am I taking more of the class time than anyone else? Am I asking questions that the professor had planned to discuss anyway? Did I jump in too soon with my question? Was my question to the point? How do the other students react when I ask a question or make a comment? Are my comments really relevant or am I just so excited about being in class that I have to say everything I can think of? Could I ask some of these questions in private? Does everyone seem to have the same question I am asking or is my problem unique and would it perhaps be more productive for the class if it were asked in private? If I had done the reading that had been assigned would I have had to ask the question?

I do not mean that you should be quiet in class and not participate. You must participate, but remember that participate means be a part of. You must be a part of the class and not take it over.

Relationship With Fellow Students

Being conscious of this will help you in establishing friendships with other students. If the class has a mixed age group you will probably first seek friendship with others who are also returning to school. Don't neglect those who are in different age groups. Younger classmates can be good friends and greatly enrich your knowledge of people. The present student body seems to be less sure that there is no life after twenty-one than it was a few years back. The pendulum is moving and the average age of the population is moving up a little every year. The baby boom is over but we are not all gray panthers yet.

The columnists who give advice often tell a person who is trying to make friends to be a good listener. This is good advice for you also. Ask to join

a group for lunch or for a walk. What are they interested in? Can you contribute? Some may not want
to hear "when I was young" but some will. You are
changing as a person. You have a double role, like
a CIA agent. By day you are a student living in a
student world (or it may be by night depending on
your schedule), and the rest of the time you are a
mature individual with a responsible role in the
community. You must use both of these aspects in
establishing new friendships.

Just as you had children or gardens or whatever
in common with your neighbors, you will have
school and teachers and assignments in common
with your classmates. These things go beyond age
and even personalities. You will find that you can
be of help to some students and others can be of
help to you. Establishing these helping relationships,
studying together for example, will help you to develop new and important friendships.

Although you may have other responsibilities
in terms of family or work or both, don't rush off
from school right after class. Don't limit your hours
at school to class hours if you can possibly help it.
If you are going to develop as a person, school must
be more than just class sessions. If your timetable
is so tight that you cannot spend a few minutes talking to a friend or looking at a book that is "only"
interesting and not a specific assignment, you are
missing a great deal.

Try to become part of the school. Try to come
to class early or even on a day when you don't have
a class and can meet with a new friend. Do not think
that the friendship aspect is foolish. It is a very important component of your act of returning and
should be treated as such.

"ACT YOUR AGE"

How often we may have said this to a youngster who was acting up! What does it mean in your case? Another adage says "you are only as old as you feel." Someplace you must achieve a balance that is satisfying to you between maintaining your adult extracurricular life and participating in school activities with classmates. You might not feel like trying out for the girl's basketball team but consider going to a game. Going to school should include some elements of fun as well as work. Even if you are on a tight schedule, try to include some fun. You may want to include your family in this fun. They might enjoy that basketball game, too, for example.

You will have a decision to make. Will you try to bring together your family and new friends or will you keep them separate? This is a decision you should make consciously. Sometimes it is better to keep them separate. Sometimes it is not.

In summary then, try to minimize stress in your life as a student and try to identify your new role. Develop friendships. Look at returning to school as far more than just going to class. Let the whole experience of school enrich your life.

PART

SKILLS FOR SURVIVAL

chapter 9

Learning to Learn

TUNING UP YOUR SKILLS

Can I Do It?

If you are thinking about returning to school this is probably your biggest question. It may be a secret question, one you are afraid to ask yourself. It is a question, however, that must be asked and the solution must be approached in a very systematic way. There are certain skills you must have if you are to be successful in returning to school, especially if you are returning to a college program.

Your ability to read and write will be key elements in your success. You will have to learn to do research papers and make effective use of the library, how to take tests, how to perfect your note-taking and outline-making techniques. Most of all you will have to learn to read better and learn to write better. You will have to learn how to learn.

Think about what you will be doing. You will have selected a program, a school, and made some accommodations in your lifestyle in order to go back to school. All of these things will be important to you. They will be on your mind when you begin your studies but do not let them deter you from one of your main activities. You will be learning. This is something you have been doing every day for many years. The difference is that you have not been conscious of the learning you have been doing. Also you have not, for the most part, been evaluated on your success in learning.

What Is Learning?

Do you remember the first time you learned to do something that was special for you. It may have been throwing a baseball, playing the piano, riding a bicycle, or driving a car. It may have been something quite different. Because it was important for you, you probably remember many of the details—who taught you, who else was there. Memory is only a part of learning. There are many levels of learning and of memory as well.

It is impossible to remember learning everything you have ever learned. Sometimes you learn in a very formal way. When the word learning was introduced, you probably thought of the classroom. This is only one way to learn, however.

One reason that you may have some insecurity is that it may have been a number of years since you were last in the classroom. Although this may be true, you have never stopped learning.

SOURCES OF LEARNING

One obvious source of learning for you may have been the newspaper. Current events were not the only things you learned. Think of the recipes you have clipped out to try at some later date, think of the gossip columns you have read, think of the sales you have pursued and the new products or styles you have learned of through newspapers and magazines.

Television

Television is another source of learning. Perhaps you have watched children's programs with your children. Have you ever thought about what the producer or writer was trying to accomplish with a particular skit for children? Sometimes the program is designed for pure entertainment. Sometimes there is a lesson hidden in the script.

There are a semi-infinite number of things to be learned from television. National Geographic specials and historical programs open up one world to us while soap operas reveal a variety of lifestyles with which (I suspect) most of us are completely unfamiliar in our lives. We learn informally, without even knowing that we are learning.

Think of all the things you learned yesterday. You would probably get tired of the task if you started to write down a list of these things. This learning was almost accidental.

It is possible for you to increase your control

of the learning process. This technique will help students do better. It will make your academic life easier and more successful.

There are those who think that learning is like breathing, something that anyone can do. In some ways this is true but in other ways it is not true. You can learn to learn better. What you need to discover is not just how to learn but how YOU learn. What is YOUR learning style?

There are some questions you must ask yourself:

1. Where do you learn best? At a desk in a quiet place? In a confortable chair? Somewhere else? What is your best learning environment?
2. When do you learn best? In the morning? In the afternoon? In the evening?
3. Do you learn better by listening or by reading? This is a very important question.
4. Do you like to read? If your answer is no, why don't you like to read? Do you read too slowly? Is reading hard for you? Are you unable to find books on topics that appeal to you?

These are questions that you must answer for yourself. There are no right or wrong answers. Draw up your profile. Are you a morning person who likes to read in a comfortable chair (I am) or are you a night person who likes to listen and write at a desk (my husband is)? What is your profile? Make use of that information in deciding when you should study and where you should study. If you are a morning person don't leave all your work until after the children are in bed at night. Instead, go to bed early and set the clock. Do your studying before your family gets up and the rest of your day starts.

Printed Material

Some people learn best from a book or a magazine, that is, from printed material. Other people learn best from their own notes. They must summarize other people's work. They find they do their best work if they make an outline of what it is they are to learn.

Tape Recorder

Some people learn best when they listen to the material they are trying to learn. For people who learn best this way, a tape recorder is a helpful tool. Sometimes it is possible to record talks or classes. Be sure to get the professor's permission to tape a class. Another helpful technique is to record your notes or selections from books onto tape and then listen to this information played back at another time. You can make use of time you have to spend waiting for someone or the time you spend driving or doing household chores by listening to your own personal "learning tapes." Even if you are not a listener by nature this technique can prove to be very useful.

Learn to learn. Learn just how you learn and make every minute of your time count. It is important that you learn to be efficient in your work. Then you will have time to do it well and still have another part to your life. That is important too. The learning years are not just a time when the clock stops. You are still a person with other aspects to your life. Very few can eliminate all other things but the school program. You are balancing many parts of your life and you will be happier if you can sharpen your learning skills.

chapter 10

Learning to Read Better

You know how to read. Of course you know how to read. You learned to do that as a little child. You may have learned to read by using whatever teaching method was popular when you went to school or whatever method you worked out for yourself. Of course you know how to read! And yet, do you really know how? Are you comfortable reading? Do you like to read? How fast do you read? What do you like to read? Do you understand everything you read? How large a vocabulary do you have? What is your speaking vocabulary? What is your reading vocabulary? These are all questions that you must answer for yourself.

EVALUATING READING ABILITY

Tests that evaluate a person's reading ability have a number of components which evaluate your reading ability according to different criteria. Reading comprehension is one of the most important. It doesn't matter how fast you read if you don't understand what you are reading. An old story comes to mind about the man in the car who had taken the wrong road. He said he was lost but he was making great time. On the other hand reading slowly does not insure that you are understanding what you are reading.

Vocabulary

Vocabulary is another element of reading to be considered. How large a reading vocabulary do you have? Every area of study has its own vocabulary—its own jargon. It is important that you understand the vocabulary of your specialty as well as the general words with which every well educated person must be familiar.

Timing

Timing is an especially important characteristic also. Do you read in phrases or only in one word bites? Reading one word at a time makes reading very much less effective. It is important to know just how you are reading now. You may never have paid any attention to how you were reading. You will have to analyze your habits. Some characteristics of reading are more easily tested than others. If you feel that you are a poor reader and have always been a poor reader it would be well for you to attend a reading clinic for awhile. You will have your problems professionally diagnosed and there will be material available to remediate your problems. The school you are planning to attend may have such a program, but such programs will also be available in community colleges and sometimes in adult education programs in your local school.

If you are not sure of your reading ability and would like to do some testing on yourself, there are several things you can evaluate.

Speed

The speed of your reading is a quality which you can test rather easily. You may have seen ads for courses known as speed reading. I am not suggesting that you become a speed reader but I am hoping that you will take some of the ideas developed for speed reading and use them to increase your effective rate of reading. Reading is the core of any college program. If you work on your reading, you are really working on all your other subjects. You learn all of your other subjects through reading. You even learn mathematics through reading, for you have to read the "theory" section in the book in order to understand the method for solving the problems.

Many techniques have been developed so that the reader can read faster with increased comprehension. It is important that you establish good reading speed. For one thing the faster you read the more you read in a certain amount of time and the more work you will get done in the amount of time you have available for doing your work. Remember that time will be a difficult commodity for you to come by.

Also, you will enjoy it more if you read faster. You will find that your return to school will be more psychologically satisfying. If you are just plodding along, you will soon get tired and discouraged. It will be too much work. Always keep in mind that when you are reading for information, your speed will vary with what you are reading. If you are reading an adventure story, you will read much faster than if you are reading a chemistry book. There is more detail to understand and learn in the science book than in the romance and it will take you much longer to do certain reading assignments than others, just because of the nature of the material.

Another factor to consider if you have any choice of book is to find one with print and page layout which are comfortable for you. If you can, choose print that is large and lines that are not too long. If you are reading a novel, you may find that a paperback version is convenient to handle and take along but you may not be able to read it as quickly as the hardbook version because the print is small and your eyes become tired more quickly.

Try some tests to see just how fast you are reading. To do this you need a timer or a watch with a second hand. Take a magazine article that has an average vocabulary and have someone time you for thirty seconds while you read at your regular reading speed. Start when they say start and stop at the end of thirty seconds. Count the number of words you read in this time. So that you don't have to count every word, you can count a few lines and determine if the number of words is almost the same for each line. Get an average value for the number of words per line by adding together the number of words in four or five lines and dividing by the number of lines counted. Multiply the total number of lines read by this average value to get the number of words read in thirty seconds, then multiply by two to obtain the number of words you read in one minute. For example, suppose the average number of words per line is 10 and you read 15 lines of the magazine, then your average reading speed would be $15 \times 10 = 150$ words for thirty seconds, $150 \times 2 = 300$ words per minute.

What does this mean? Is your result fast or slow? Is it good? It is hard to give an exact answer to the question of rate. One important variable in the question is the type of material and the understanding you have of your material. For adults with material which has an "average" vocabulary and not too much detail to study, the following scale seems to be fairly useful:

200 wpm or below	poor
300 wpm	average
400 wpm	very good
over 500	outstanding

If you come out high on the scale when you do your own reading speed count, you may consider this to be good. If you don't come out as well as you would like, you should include increasing your speed as one of your objectives in the personal reading program you will draw up for yourself.

Practice

Practicing reading, like so many other parts of learning, really does help. Whether you come out high or low on the scale you can always improve. The important thing to measure will be how much you can improve your own reading ability, and some of this will be measured by your speed.

If you are going to improve your speed, you must

find out just what it is that is slowing you down. Knowing how to read each word is only one part of reading. Another part is how you put the words you are reading together. If you read one word at a time, it will take you longer to read the sentence. You might say that you are reading for understanding, but much of the understanding comes from putting the words together. If you read one word at a time you will find yourself forgetting what the sentence says before you finish reading the words. Learn to read a couple of words at a time, read whole phrases. Gradually you will find yourself gulping down whole sentences.

If you had a serving of peas and you tried eating them one at a time you would soon become tired of eating peas and you wouldn't really get the taste of them either. You have to take a few at a time, a spoonful or forkful perhaps, to get the full flavor of the peas. You also have to learn to take into yourself a full serving of words at a time. This helps you to read faster and with more understanding. It also increases your pleasure in reading.

One rather obvious thing to be considered is your eyesight. If you are planning to return to school, you will be making considerable use of your eyes. You say you are always using your eyes now but in reality you probably have not been doing the concentrated reading you will find yourself doing once you return to school. If you have not had your eyes checked in a while it would be advisable to consider doing this. You may have a problem that you haven't noticed because you were not using your eyes to the degree that you will be using them in college work. Even if you are seeing properly, there are many ways in which your eyes can slow you down in your reading, or in which they can be trained to speed it up.

CORRECTING READING FAULTS

One way that people are slowed down is to let the eye go back over what has been read before. It is very difficult to know you are doing this. Special cameras are used to detect the eye movement. In younger children the eye is likely to travel back over the word that has been read. This is part of the developmental process in children and part of the determination of reading readiness. It is as though you were reading just like this like this this. You can see how many words you are reading. By letting your eye travel back over the page, you are increasing the total number of words that you are reading and reducing comprehension. Becoming aware of the fact that you may be doing this seems to help get rid of the problem. There is no real test for it that you could make up, but try to notice if you are doing this and force yourself on to the next word without going back. Being aware of the problem seems to help correct it.

Unconsciously Sounding Words

Just as your eyes are involved with reading, your voice is also involved. Some people are very verbal and they demonstrate this even when they read. Some people unconsciously make sounds, others do not make a noise but do move their lips, still others seem to "activate" their vocal cords without actually making a sound.

To see the difference this can make, take a short

paragraph and time yourself while you read it silently. Read the same paragraph out loud and time yourself. You will see how much longer it takes you to read it out loud even though you have already read it to yourself and know what words are coming. Run your fingers over your lips as you read a paragraph to yourself and see if they are moving. If there is some slight movement, you can practice to get rid of this habit by keeping a finger on your lips for awhile until there is no hint of movement when you read.

More difficult to discover is an action which involves using your vocal cords as if you were going to sound the word but never actually move your lips. This is very hard to find but sometimes if you hit a barrier at about 300 wpm it may be because of this habit. Again, knowing or suspecting that you are doing it is sometimes a help in overcoming the problem.

The secret to reading faster with good understanding is practice. To practice correctly, you must push yourself. You are already reading at a certain rate. If you read at the same rate it will not really help you to read faster. Select a book, set aside 10 minutes a day and see how fast you can read with good understanding. Keep a record of how many words per minute you are reading each day. The book will have the same number of words on a page (on the average). Select a magazine and do the same with it for 10 minutes if you prefer. The magazine will give you practice with the shorter line. Since the eye will not do so much traveling, you will generally read faster on the magazine page. Have someone time you at the end of your reading session to get a word-per-minute entry for your record if you can.

Otherwise use a timer for the 10-minute period and divide the total number of words read by 10 to get your word-per-minute entry.

PACING

Pacing is another way to improve your reading rate. This means that you try to read a certain amount in a certain period of time. It should be quite a bit more than you normally read. After pacing yourself in this way for awhile, you will find that you reach your goal quite regularly. Then set another goal. By doing this, your regular reading rate will become greater. Part of it comes from being aware of what you are doing while you are reading, part from getting rid of bad habits, and part from actual physical practice.

Do not fool yourself into thinking you are reading faster if you are understanding less. You should really be understanding more. A later section discusses the art of skimming which is very useful when you have a lot of material that must be looked at in a short time. The next section discusses your depth of understanding of the material you are reading.

READING COMPREHENSION

The term reading comprehension includes several things. A first thing to consider is why you are reading this particular piece of material. Is it for entertainment, for instruction, for very specific detail? If you are reading a receipe or a set of instructions for assembling something, you may have to read and reread the piece several times. You may have to read it step by step as you follow the instructions. If you are reading a mystery or adventure story, you may read very quickly, trying to get to the conclusion, absorbing the feeling and the details of the material without being able to repeat any of it exactly. If you are studying a text, you will have to be able to repeat details, opinions, perhaps names and dates. The type of material dictates your approach to comprehension.

One basic element in comprehension is determining the main idea of the selection which you are reading. Begin with a paragraph-by-paragraph analysis. What is the main idea of the paragraph? If you had to tell it in a few words what would they be? If you are having trouble with the paragraph, try analyzing it sentence-by-sentence. You must be able to rephrase and select. You must be able to spotlight what is important. What is the author trying to say? After you are able to identify the main idea of the paragraph, try identifying the main ideas of a larger piece of work. If the work is very detailed, what are the details you must remember?

Tests which evaluate your reading ability have sections that evaluate your comprehension. Comprehension is related to retention. Comprehension measures what you understand and retention measures how long you remember it. If you do not thoroughly understand something, you will not remember it very well.

Comprehension Tests

The comprehension sections of tests instruct you to read a selection and then respond to questions. These tests report the results in a number of different ways, one of which is a grade level. If you are evaluated on one of these tests, you may get some idea of your reading level. You should not feel that tests are absolutely accurate or completely dependable, but they will give you a general feeling for your competency.

There are a number of ways you can get an idea of your comprehension level without putting a "number" or grade level on it. Try and get a number of children's school books. Social studies might be a good subject to begin with. If you are a history buff, don't use an area or a period of history with which you are familiar as the basis for your reading. You will not be measuring your comprehension but your ability to remember facts you knew before you read the material. Take a book, preferably a high school book, and read a section. Then turn to the questions at the end of the chapter. Can you answer them without referring to the material in the chapter?

Take a magazine article and read it. Can you make up a new title for the article which summarizes the main idea or ideas into a few words? What was the main idea? Summarize the main points the author made. Were there important names, dates, or places mentioned? Practice doing this, even with the newspaper. This is best done with a friend who will judge whether you are getting the "right answers." If you have difficulties in this area that do not seem to be corrected by the things that you can do yourself, you probably should seek some time in a reading clinic. Although it may seem to be an expense in terms of both time and money, it will help you to be successful in achieving your primary goal. Without it you may have great difficulty in staying in school and getting satisfactory grades.

If you are setting aside time to do an assignment, you will have to make allowance for the difficulty of the material and the amount of detail in it. Reading specialists have developed a number of tests which they "give" to material to determine its "readibility." The tests consist of looking at the material and determining the vocabulary level and the number of syllables in words and words per sentence. If you are able to select your own material for a particular assignment you might want to be conscious of these factors.

Do you feel confident in reading certain complex sentences if the vocabulary is not too difficult? A later section will discuss techniques for increasing your reading vocabulary. You will probably have a much larger reading vocabulary than speaking vocabulary. You will recognize words and know the meaning of many words which you would not consider using in your day-to-day conversation.

Detailed Comprehension

If you are doing study-type reading, you are trying to be aware of detail. It is almost impossible to learn all the detail on a first reading. The best approach is to read the material quickly, almost superficially, to get a broad overview. Then reread the material with attention to detail. The third step is to make notes about the important facts you need to learn from the material you have read. If you try to learn the detail on the first reading, you will not be able to determine just what is important and may find yourself recopying every sentence and calling each "important." A quick overview will permit you to evaluate the material and determine just what you must learn from it.

If you are too tired when you are trying to read, you may be just wasting your time. Be conscious of whether or not you are really understanding what you are reading. If you are, you will be able to re-phrase the material. If you are alone, try saying out loud just what you have read in your own words. If you are with others—for example, in a library—you won't be able to do this. You will have to do it mentally.

Comprehension is the most important part of reading. If you don't understand what you are reading, you won't remember the important material.

THE ART OF SKIMMING

Skimming is a technique which will help you cut down on the amount of material you have to read. In the process of doing a paper or writing a report, you will find more material than will actually be useful to you. Even after you have eliminated those books and articles which are not really relevant, you may still have a great deal to read. When you use the technique of skimming, you get a lot of information without really reading it all.

If you were to set a stone skimming across the surface of a lake you would see that stone cut straight across, possibly jumping a little, touching only a little of the surface and reaching its final destination in a very short time. When you skim in a book, you act, in a way, as though the material isn't there.

Skimming is both an art and a technique to be developed. You may be skimming an index, a table of contents, or a chapter in a book. First you must decide exactly what you are looking for. You must then decide on a list of key words which are related to your final objectives. Your eye then travels down the page looking for these key words which open up the key ideas. If you are working with an index or a table of contents, the eye can travel directly along it. If you are looking at a closely spaced piece of written material, let your eye begin at the top left and travel diagonally across the page to the bottom right looking for the flags you have selected as the key words. These flags tell you to stop and look more closely at the material in that place.

Getting the Main Idea

Usually the opening sentence in a paragraph tells the main idea of the paragraph. Learning to skim can help you save time and energy and do a much better report. Take a look at some different pieces of written material. Practice skimming the material and then read it. See if you can find a way of getting information without having to read everything.

Usually, if the material is well written, the first sentence in the paragraph gives you information about what the paragraph will contain. If the first sentence doesn't do it, either the second or the last one will. You can use these pieces of information to check to see if the paragraph is going to tell you what you need to know. Something of the same approach can be used for chapters in books. Skimming is a technique for maximizing the results of your reading efforts.

1. Take a book you have found on one of your topics. Use the key words you have made up and skim the index for these words. Then read the index and see if you have gotten all the references. Do this several times with other books.

2. Take a chapter in a book and quickly skim the beginning, middle, and end of the chapter and

write down what you learned. Read those same sections over and see if you did get the meaning from what you skimmed.

BUILDING YOUR VOCABULARY

Everybody has two vocabularies, a reading vocabulary and a speaking vocabulary. You might add a third—a writing vocabulary. You recognize the meaning of many words which you would not use in ordinary conversation. If you are going to increase your reading power and your potential for college work, you must increase all of your vocabularies. If you concentrate on your reading vocabulary, you will find that the other two will be increased through the new words you will come to know and through the new experiences and new responsibilities you will have to meet.

One way to increase your vocabulary is by being conscious of words. Words are the things you are reading. Words have meanings, of course, but they also have histories and relationships. Some words have several meanings which are different. Some words have a very rich history. If you are conscious of words, you will be taking the first step toward building your vocabulary.

Keeping Notes

Buy a small notebook that you will designate as your vocabulary-building notebook. When I read a Russian novel (in translation, of course, like Tolstoy's Anna Karenina) I find myself skipping names of people and places. My eye develops a sense of the pattern of the letters so that I know what is happening to whom but I am not really conscious of how to say the names correctly. If I were asked to repeat the names of the characters in the book, I probably would not be able to do it. You may be doing the same thing with words you do not know when you read. You may be missing the meaning of the sentence or even skipping whole sentences because you do not know the meaning of a word or a few words. At times it is possible to understand what is being said because of the context in which the word is used, but even then you are slowed down. Your rhythm of reading, your pattern, has been broken.

Use the notebook to write down words you come across which you cannot easily define. A dictionary is an important tool, but you are not likely to look up every word you don't know at the time you first read it. This process would slow your studying down so much that you would lose the thread of what you were actually doing. If you are reading from one of your own books you can make a little check mark and return to the page later to transfer the word into your notebook.

After you have entered your "new" word, make a guess at the meaning of the word. Try using it in a sentence. Then look it up in the dictionary. A few hints for using your dictionary will be given later but be aware of the different meanings of the word. Try using the word in a sentence. How close were you? Are there other words which have the same root, the same origin? This is how your vocabulary-building has an opportunity to branch out.

Dictionaries

The dictionary is an important tool and should be selected so that you are comfortable using it. A huge, heavy book containing very fine print might have a great many words in it but be seldom used because it is inconvenient. A dictionary that is of a size and, most importantly, has a type face size that is comfortable for YOU is the one you should buy. If you find a small paperback to be best, don't be ashamed of it. You are using it. You are building yourself and your vocabulary from it. When you are not able to find the words you are seeking in your dictionary, the time has come to purchase a second one.

A few words on the use of the dictionary might be helpful here. I must admit that I am interested in words and often stray from the path of looking up a certain word to wander among other interesting words on the page. This is not necessarily a bad habit, but it does slow you down.

Dictionaries are set up a little differently, but many have two words written at the top of every page. The word on the left indicates the first word on the page, while the word on the right indicates the last word on the page. If the word you are seeking is alphabetically between the two words, it will be found on that page if the dictionary contains a definition of the word you are seeking. To decide if a word is alphabetically between the two words, you must look at the word you are seeking and decide if the letters come after the first word and before the letters of the second word in the order of presentation. The dictionary will also include a key to pronunciation which will help you to increase your speaking vocabulary.

There are two categories of words you will be working with. One is general words, the other is words that belong to a certain area of study, for example scientific terms. It is important to realize that there are many kinds of dictionaries which focus on words from certain areas. Some dictionaries include the origin and the history of the word.

A word is not really "yours" until you can use it comfortably. Keep reviewing, keep adding words to your recognition vocabulary, and then add those words to your spoken vocabulary or written vocabulary. Set a goal for each day. Will you learn one new word, really learn it? That is 365 words in a year! Can you learn two or three? That's not too many, is it? Vocabulary building is a step-by-step process that goes along with pacing your reading, increasing your speed, and deepening your comprehension.

Look through the books you will be using and identify words that you are not comfortable with. Let yourself develop the habit of adding words to your "look-up list."

Become word conscious. Become aware of words. Spend some time wandering in the dictionary. Return to words that you have put on your list and see if you can still define them. If you are not sure, check the word list again and review the definition you wrote down. Try using the word in a sentence.

Increasing your vocabulary, especially your reading vocabulary, will make you more comfortable in your classes. You will better understand what your teachers are saying to you. As you write papers and tests you will have a richer set of words to use in the preparation of your material. You will feel more confident in your presentations in class and in your out-of-class conversations as well.

Speech is the measure of an educated person. Increasing your vocabulary is something that you can do on your own. It requires steady application of your time and effort. There are a number of paperback books on the market which have vocabularies grouped together. These books can be time-savers for you. Another aspect of increasing your vocabulary is to be aware of "root" words and prefixes and endings.

Improving Spelling

Improving your spelling seems to go hand in hand with improving your vocabulary. Although reading is the topic we are discussing, a moment spent on spelling fits in here. English is a difficult language when it comes to spelling.

Certain letters have certain primary or basic phonetic sound but they are only used in words about twenty per cent of the time. The rest of the time other combinations of letters produce that sound. This makes it very difficult to spell "naturally." Identify words that are commonly misspelled. Do you have problems with them? There are rules for endings which you can learn. Again there are books that help you to learn certain types of words. Roots are important in spelling as they are in vocabulary-building. Make a list of words which are difficult for you to remember how to spell. Keep adding to the list and also keep subtracting from the list as you become confident in your spelling of the words.

chapter 11

The Art of Taking a Test

The word "test" can cause spine-tingling chills for some people, while others seem to be able to stay calm and do well on tests. If you belong to the first group, try working on this section and turn yourself into a member of the second group.

Taking a test is not really a part of learning. Sometimes though, you do learn that you may not have learned what you thought you had learned. Test-taking is at the end of so many learning experiences that it seems a good idea to give some ways of making it a little less painful.

One of the first things to do is believe the person who is giving the test. Quite often, teachers will tell you what material will be covered by the test and what format the test will have. They may tell you if you are to have multiple choice questions, problems, or some combination of question types. You have to believe that the teacher really wants to find out if you have learned the material. The questions are not to trick you. They are to test you.

MAKING UP YOUR OWN TESTS

The next thing to do is to go through the material to be covered on the real test and practice by MAKING UP YOUR OWN TESTS. You know how long you will have to take the test. Perhaps it will be fifteen minutes, or forty-five minutes or two hours. It is a fixed length of time. Perhaps you know the type of questions. Go through the pages that you have to cover and make up questions from the different sections. Some questions may draw several sections together. Try to make up questions that show the most important points in the section you have read. After you have made up the questions for each section, select some of the questions and put them together to make up a test. Remember the test should cover topics from most of the material you have studied. It should also be possible to take it in the amount of time you will be allowed for the real test. Make up at least three complete tests.

Taking Your Own Tests

The third step is to TAKE THE TESTS THAT YOU MAKE UP. Everybody practices everything—sports, music, painting—but very few people practice taking tests. For most people, every test that they take is the real thing. They never are able to relax and figure out just what is the best procedure for test-taking *for them* because so much depends on every test they take. Practice taking tests. Give yourself tests. Time them. Correct them. You will do better when the time comes to take the real test. This will be partly because you will be relaxed and not so scared and partly because, through taking the tests, you will have learned the material.

Attitude is a very important thing when you take a test. If you are afraid either of taking the test or of the results of your grade on the test you will find it harder to do well. It is natural to be scared but you can learn to remove some of your fears through planning.

USING TEST TIME EFFECTIVELY

Time is one of the most important parts of a test. You can plan your time. Suppose there are five questions and you have thirty-five minutes to finish the test. If you divide thirty-five minutes by five questions you would find that you have seven minutes, on the average, to answer each question if you are to finish right on time. If you spend a little more time on one question, then you will have to take time from the other questions. This is a decision you have to make but make sure you do make it. Don't just let the time get away from you and leave a question that you could have answered undone because you ran out of time. Most rooms in which you take tests have a clock but if this is not the case, a watch becomes very important to you. Never take a test without having some way to keep track of your time.

Another thing that you can change is the order in which you do the questions. Sometimes a teacher requires you to do the questions in a certain order. You must do question one first then question two, etc. Other times you can do them in different orders because you fill in your answers on the test paper. As long as you put the right answers in the right spaces, no one is going to know that you filled in the answer to question seven before you did question two. Sometimes a teacher will allow you to do the test in a different order as long as it is clearly marked.

Look over the test when you get it. Do this quickly because you may find yourself short of time later. See if there is a question that you can answer immediately. If so, do it. Make a little note next to some of the questions with an idea for the answer. Sometimes, under the pressure of actually completing the exam, you can forget an answer you knew when you first looked at the test paper. Why should you do the questions you can answer first? This gives you confidence, makes you feel good, so you relax and do better on the rest of the test. If you are in doubt about which question to do next, do the one with most credit attached, if you know both answers.

Selecting Test Questions

One of the most important things is to read the directions carefully. If you have a choice of questions— for example, "Do seven questions" might be the instruction—put a big number on the top of your page to remind you how many questions you have to do. Go down the list of questions and put a check mark next to the ones you can do best. If you do not find seven questions that you can do best, do the ones you feel confident in before trying to select the others. Be very careful to leave enough time for the remaining questions. Why do it this way, rather than select all the questions at once? The answer is that doing the ones you are sure of may give you enough confidence to do well on the others. Don't spend all day trying to decide which questions to pick. Use your time to best advantage. Always try and relax. Sometimes you know more than you think you know. Of course, it is true that sometimes you know less, but why talk about that?

TIPS ON STUDYING FOR A TEST

Time is also important when you are studying for a test. Before the test is to be given, divide up the amount of time you will have and the sections you have to cover. Remember that some sections may be more difficult than others, so divide up the time accordingly. Don't use it all in going through the material for the first time. Leave some for review and for taking the tests that you make up.

Come to the test early and find a seat where you will be comfortable. If you use a fountain pen or ball-point, make sure you have enough ink or a refill. If you use pencils, make sure you have several sharpened. Don't use precious test time sharpening pencils. Make sure you mark each problem or question so that the person correcting it can find it. If you get an answer for a problem, put a box around that final answer so that it can be found easily by the person correcting the exam. Be as neat as you can.

If you prepare well, you will be relaxed enough to do well on your tests.

chapter 12

How to Survive Doing a Paper

"I've got a paper to do" is the plaintive cry of all college students at one time or another. As a returning student, you will find yourself faced with many assignments of "papers."

What is this paper that causes such turmoil in the hearts of students? Generally it is a report in which you present ideas and draw on the research and opinions of others to support those ideas or topics.

There are several steps you have to follow when doing a paper:

1. choose a topic
2. establish a timetable
3. obtain and use the research materials
4. record and make notes on material
5. find a pivotal point of view
6. write the paper

7. prepare the footnotes and bibliography
8. type the paper

Although they are obviously connected, let us look at the steps one at a time.

CHOOSE A TOPIC

There are times when a professor will assign specific topics or even a very specific title for your paper. You may feel that you are being confined intellectually by such an assignment. In most of these cases, you should feel relieved. The professor generally gives you titles or topics that he feels can be done. Topics for which there is enough research material hopefully will be on the list.

Topics are not always so easy to come by. In general, you do not have a background in the subject. You may not know what materials are available, etc. If, however, you must decide on a topic for a paper, do so only after you have taken a look at what is available in terms of published material. In order to produce a successful paper, make your final decision only after you find a central idea or focus for it, one which is exciting to you.

Facts and Opinions

It is possible to write a paper that is just a collection of facts and opinions of others but it will not be a good paper. It will not "work" as a paper. Think of it in these terms. Suppose you wrote a quotation or a summary for each of the things you have read on a file card and suppose you connected each of your cards or references with a safety pin. Suppose you handed in the whole collection of things tied together with safety pins. Probably you think that that is a ridiculous visual image I am presenting to you, but many papers are put together in just that way (sans safety pins). You need to put something of yourself in as connectors and you need to have a main idea or focus. Do not confuse this focus or point on which the paper turns with the general topic area.

Some papers are based on specific facts. You may have carried out the research study yourself and are now putting your data (facts) together, or you may be bringing together facts which were presented by other persons in other papers or reports. Other papers are based on opinion. The opinion may be yours or you may be giving the opinions of other individuals. It is important to be able to distinguish between fact and opinion when you are putting together a paper of your own.

Unfortunately, much that is presented as fact is really opinion. Do not feel that a paper based on opinion is not good. Some successful papers have been concerned with reviewing or discussing the validity of contrasting opinions on a topic held by various groups of individuals. Other papers contain only the opinions of the author, developed in a clear, thoughtful manner. There is nothing wrong with papers based on opinion if it is quite clear to the reader that the author realizes that this is opinion, not fact.

Choosing a topic is perhaps the most important part of doing a paper. If you can get the right topic, the paper may almost write itself!

Let us suppose you have a list of acceptable topics. Do you have any information, enthusiasm, or prior experience with any of the topics? As the kids would say, "Do any of the topics turn you on?" If

there is such a topic, determine if you can get enough
material to turn your ideas into an outstanding paper. Plan your paper so that you have a good chance
of getting an "A" for it. Think about what the professor is asking you to do when you give your paper.
If you have some moral problem with the topic and
want to use the paper as a vehicle to argue a point
with the professor, you have a right to do that. Do
not expect that you will get an "A" however. People
act differently when confronted with an antagonistic
paper. If you do not have such a point, try and find
out what type of paper the teacher (professor) re-
spects and give him or her the kind of paper he or
she wants. The professor usually wants a paper that
has a professional quality to it. This is highlighted
by its organization. If the topic is such that it cannot
follow an organized form or there is very little organized material available, consider seriously whether
or not you should do that topic.

If you are not comfortable with the topic, you
really can't write an outstanding paper. Very often,
especially in large classes, your image (and reputation and grade) is made with a paper. If you find
that the topic you are working on is not going right,
consider beginning another topic. It may save you
both time and your grade in the long run.

ESTABLISH A TIMETABLE

Papers turn out poorly when you don't have time
to write them. Yes, you have a number of classes
and a number of assignments, but some careful planning can keep you from burning the midnight oil
and handing in a piece of work that is thrown together at the last minute. Don't ever hand in a paper

late unless you have some extraordinary reason. Believe me, most professors have heard every excuse you could possibly invent and most of them will discount that excuse. What you are doing is placing an unnecessary amount of "spotlight" on your work. It will be viewed at a different time and with a different attitude from the other papers in the class. Do you really want that to happen? Very rarely can it be helpful to the review of your work or to your grade. If you have been in an automobile accident or a tornado, maybe—but it is best to plan ahead so that you can get your work in early or at least on time.

How long a paper are you planning to write? How long will it take you to type the final copy? Will you write out your draft or do a rough typing of it? I prefer typing myself. How many trips will you have to make to the library? How many different libraries will you have to visit? Plan to do this early. Other people will be doing papers, not necessarily in your class, and the books may be gone if you wait too long.

Set a Deadline

Minimize the time you must spend taking notes. Use the xerox machine if it is available. You may find that the time you save will be worth the additional costs. Make use of the "cut and paste" method of assembling a paper in draft form to save some time. If you do this economizing, how much time will it take you to get going? What will happen if you cannot get the material you need? How much extra time will you need if you change a topic? What if some family emergency comes up? Plan so that you will have your paper finished at least a week before it is due. That will help to relieve the pressure on you. Make a list of the tasks you must do to get your paper into final form and construct a timetable for yourself. Keep to these deadlines or else keep ahead of them. As you do papers, you will learn to have good predictabilities with respect to your deadlines. Deadlines are really lifelines!

OBTAIN AND USE THE RESEARCH MATERIALS

You may find as a returnee that your home-away-from-home is the library and your best friends are the librarians who can find the material you need. If the library is to be of much use to you, you must know what it has and what it does not have. You must determine its hours and policies and how they will effect you. Make your own map of the library, marking the different things that are of interest to you. What is a microfiche? Can you use one? What kind of materials does the library have available on microfilm and what can it order? Can you order materials from other libraries through your library? What will it cost? Can you use the libraries at other colleges in the neighborhood or even in the next city? Does your student card permit you to use certain collections of other libraries? All these things are possible. Find out how things are for your situation. Does the library have a xerox machine? What coin or coins does it take. Invest in a roll of them and take them with you when you go to the library. Sometimes it is impossible to get change just when you need it most.

Libraries have many different opportunities for study. Some libraries have extensive reserve collections or reference collections. Some faculty members put books that you will need for your course work "on reserve" at the beginning of the year. These books can then be used only in the library or can be taken out on very limited loan (such as overnight or on the weekends). While this may seem limiting, it gives all the students in the class an opportunity to use the material, rather than allowing the first student to the library the opportunity to take it all.

Reference Materials

Reference materials may include rare volumes as well as encyclopedias, dictionaries, and other reference materials. There arc dictionaries of special topics such as science, music, and art, as well as ones which concern themselves with words and their origins. There are a great number of encyclopedias published which (in spite of the claims of the editors) don't really vary very much. If you have found a fairly substantial entry on your topic in one encyclopedia, you probably won't add much to your knowledge base by reviewing another encyclopedia for its entry on the subject, unless there is some specific fact neglected by the first which you feel the second volume will give you. Go instead to some book which will give you a more in-depth study of your topic.

The organization of books in the library may confuse you at first. Suppose you had a great many books. You could divide them in many ways—by author, by topic, by age, by color of binding, or by size. Many of these divisions would be of more use than others. If you are using your books as room decorations, color might make the most sense—if you don't ever read them! The library itself does some division by size. They make their bookshelves an average size and any books that are larger must go to the oversized section. Books are generally divided first by topic or kind of book and then by author.

Although some libraries are putting the records of their collection on microfilm, many still use the card system. Careful study of the card or microfilm entry can give you a great deal of information and may help you limit the number of books you have to read. Some sample cards are given below and on the following pages.

Fodor's Brazil.
New York, David McKay Co.

    v. ill. 19 cm. annual. (Fodor's modern guides)

    Key title: Fodor's Brazil, ISSN 0163–0628

    1. Brazil—Description and travel—1951— —Guide-books.
I. Title: Brazil.

F2509.5.F62   918.1'04'6   78–645653
                                                                   MARC-S

Library of Congress   78

Tindemans, Leo.
    Speech at the National Press Club luncheon, Washington,
Oct. 21, 1977. [Sound recording]
    1 reel. 3¾ ips. mono. 7 in.

    Reel 806.
    Originally broadcast over National Public Radio.
    SUMMARY: Prime Minister of Belgium Leo Tindemans, the
first prime minister to visit the United States since 1937, speaks
of his country as a meeting place for nations and emphasizes
his advocacy of European unity.

    1. Belgium—Foreign relations—1914—   —Addresses, es-
says, lectures.   2. European Federation—Addresses, essays,
lectures.   I. National Press Club of Washington, Washington, D.C.

[DH692.T.A5–59]   78–741608

Library of Congress   78   MN

Simple equations. [Videorecording]/United States Department
of the Air Force.—Washington: The Dept.: distributed by National Audiovisual Center, 1978.

    1 cassette, 40 min.: sd., b&w; ¾ in.

    U standard.
    Previously issued as 16 mm. motion picture.
    SUMMARY: Explains axioms and algebraic rules needed
to solve simple linear equations.

    1. Equations—Numerical solutions. I. United States.
Dept. of the Air Force.

[QA218]   512.9   78–706291
                                                   MARC
National Audiovisual
Center
for Library of Congress   79   F

```
Richards, Peter G
    The reformed local government system/by Peter G. Rich-
ards.—3d ed., rev.—London; Boston: G. Allen & Unwin, 1978.

    192 p.; 22 cm.—(New local government series; 5)    GB***
Bibliography: p. [185]–186.
Includes index.
ISBN 0–04–352068–5




    1. Local government—Great Britain.   I. Title.

JS3095 1978.R5   1978              352.042            78–319616
                                                      MARC
    Library of Congress            79
```

The cards are filed in cabinets or are filed in alphabetical order according to author, book title, and subject matter. Check the date of publication to determine if the material is current. The summary will provide you with some information. From this you may be able to determine whether or not the book will suit your needs.

There are a number of different filing systems which make use of different categories of numbers and letters to separate the books. These numbers are printed at the bottom of the cards. The first set of numbers refers to the category of the book in the Library of Congress system, while the second set refers to the listing of the book in the Dewey Decimal system. The third number is the number by which you order the card. University libraries often use the Library of Congress system, while many public libraries use the Dewey Decimal system. Discover the system your library uses and make or copy a floor plan indicating where different categories of books may be found.

In addition to books, libraries have collections of audiovisual materials. Films and records may be checked out just as books are. Libraries often make use of microfilm to expand their collections. Many people feel insecure, at first, in using the microfilm readers. Microfiche is somewhat easier to use but many journals are still using microfilm. Ask someone to help you with the machine until you learn to use it. Don't feel self-conscious. Everyone had to learn to use it sometime.

The Reader's Guide to Periodical Literature will provide you with listings of magazine and journal articles. A selection from this book can be found on the next page. You can see that the range of topics is very large.

Many specialized areas of study (for example, education and science) have publications which list articles that have been published that year. Libraries keep these publications bound together for many years so that you can trace the work published on different topics for a long period of time.

An abstract is a short summary of a paper or article. There are publications which print abstracts of articles so that you can see from the abstract whether the article will serve your needs. Abbreviations of the journals are generally given at the beginning of the volume for each year.

Many libraries also have policies of interlibrary loans arranged with other libraries. There are different ways in which this works. Sometimes you pay for photocopies of materials such as journal articles.

CHILDREN—*Continued*
Social and economic status
See also
Socially handicapped children
Speech
See Children—Language
Surgery
Now, they are two; separation surgery for the Rodriguez twins. M. Gunther. il Todays Health 53:24–9+ Ja. '75
Training
See Children—Management and training
Vision
See Vision
China (People's Republic)
Green heart: notes on children's cultural activities in China. J. C. Giblin. il Horn Bk 51:564–70 D '75
Indochina
UNICEF gives aid without political discrimination in Indo-China. il UN Mo Chron 12:27–31 My '75
Northern Ireland
Mum, people go everywhere here without fighting: U.S. farm families help kids. J. Hoffman. il Farm J 99:A6–7 Ap '75
Underdeveloped areas
See Underdeveloped areas—Children
United States
Do Americans really like children? K. Keniston. il Todays Educ 64:16–21 N '75
Growing up in America—then and now. R. Coles. il por Time 106:27–9 D 29 '75
How young America lives, holiday time: 1975. il Ladies Home J 92:37–44 D '75
Pros and cons of city life for kids. N. Hentoil. il Parents Mag 51:42–3+ Ja '76
See also
Negro children
Vietnam (Republic)
See also
Vietnamese war. 1957- —Children
CHILDREN: story. See Vivante. A.
CHILDREN, adopted
Adopted child has a right to know everything. L. Dusky. il pors Parents Mag 50:40–3+ O '75
Adopted daughter meets her natural mother; excerpt from Twice born: memoirs of an adopted daughter. B. J. Lifton. il Ms 4:23–4+ D '75

In other cases, the original book is sent for a small fee. If you need some material, be sure to inquire about the interlibrary loan policy. Some very small libraries have this service available as well as large university libraries.

chapter 13

Using Your Research Material

You have now selected your topic and found some reference material. You may have found books, magazine articles, encyclopedias, and perhaps even films. What will you do with the material? Now is the point at which you must organize. You can spend a great deal of time copying material from the original source to a card or a piece of paper but this is seldom the best method. What you need to do is to develop a kind of "road map" through the material you have obtained. You will have to settle on the focus of your paper. As you review material, give it a priority number. You may not be able to read everything you have found. When you first select the material, make a quick appraisal as to its usefulness. Number your references and place the bibliographic information on separate file cards. This will be invaluable later when you are trying to do your bibliography and footnotes. On the same card make very brief notes as to the pages in the book or article which have information you will use in your paper.

Selecting Materials

Since you can't have time to read or even look at everything that was written about your subject, you must learn to be selective. You will have to determine the level of the book. Some books are written so that only an advanced researcher can read them. Other books are written for the newcomer in the field. Remember that while you may start with the newcomer books, you are going back to school to learn. Stretch your mind a little. Work your way up to the more advanced books.

If you have selected a set of books from the library, how do you know which one to use? Begin by arranging the books in front of you from simplest to the most difficult. You can begin by looking at the size of the type and the format of the book. The author's introduction is also helpful.

Review the books to see if they contain material that you need but do not already know. This information must be written in a form that you can understand. Read this material thoroughly and take notes. Take some simpler notes on the material that you already know, since you may need to include that in your report. Books that are way over your head should be avoided until you can handle them. The best reference will begin with what you already know and bring you into new material so that you understand it.

USING QUOTED MATTER

One of the problems that students have concerns the question of quoting. If you use the exact words or almost the exact words of an author, you *must* use quotation marks or somehow indicate that you have taken the material from someone else's work. To neglect to do so is to commit plagiarism. This is a very serious breach of academic form. In some cases, it may mean that you automatically fail the project or the course. At times, it is grounds for dismissal from a program. You have actually stolen someone else's work.

A situation which is not as easily understood by students is one in which a person's ideas are used without reference. The exact words may never be used, yet the material must be referenced. Ideas are important—valuable. Question yourself closely when you are putting your paper together to determine if the ideas are truly your own or if they are so closely related to what you have read that you must give credit to someone else. Remember that giving credit to someone else does not weaken your own work. Do not be guilty, however, of producing a paper that is only a string of quotations.

If you have not settled on a specific topic, you may have to do a broad range of reading. Find a manner that is convenient for you for recording the ideas and references that you are reading without writing everything down.

One thing that you must do to have a successful paper is make an outline. The sooner you make an outline, the more direction you can give to your reading and research work.

HOW TO MAKE AN OUTLINE

The outline that you make for your paper is really the skeleton of your work. If the skeleton is weak, if the parts do not work together, the body of the paper that you try to create upon it will not succeed. The outline is the plan for your paper. In simplest terms, it must have a beginning, a middle, and an end.

That seems like a simple enough statement until you start reading papers and projects and realize how many do leave out one of these parts. Certainly the paper begins and ends and has something in the middle but each of these parts must carry a certain message that you are trying to create with your work.

The Beginning

The beginning sets the tone for the paper. It tells the reader the main idea and introduces the topic to the reader. The reader doesn't know just what approach the writer will use. This must be a part of the beginning of the paper. Unfortunately the writer may be confused, not really having settled on a specific topic, although he or she has begun to write and, indeed, may have finished writing the paper. Sometimes not only does the reader get lost before the paper is finished, but the writer is also lost.

State your question or your topic clearly. Give a summary of the steps you will use to explore the topic if that is appropriate. It sometimes is and it sometimes is not. You will begin to be sensitive to this as you develop your own confidence and style.

The Middle

The middle part of the paper is where the information is given and the points really made. The author needs to construct a plan for this part. The main idea must have supporting stages. These become subheadings in the paper. If actual subheadings are not appropriate in the final document, they should at least be present in your outline. If there are several ideas to be presented, there will be a need for several subheadings under each main heading.

The End

The end of the paper is also something which must be taken seriously. Every paper ends by virtue of the fact that it stops. What is important is that the reader has the feeling that the paper really ended, not just stopped. Have you ever read something and looked for another page? The ideas were not drawn to conclusions. The work was not really finished. The author must remember to tie up all those loose ends of ideas which may have been introduced in various parts of the paper. He or she should summarize the paper, telling in brief form just what he or she was trying to do in the paper. The major focus should be repeated.

It seems as though you are doing a great deal of extra work when you carefully prepare your outline. This is not the case. You are really saving yourself time and effort in the actual writing of your paper. If material is missing, you will discover that as you prepare your outline. If your point is weak, which would ultimately result in a poor paper, that will become evident also. Skipping an outline is never a shortcut.

HOW TO TAKE NOTES AND USE THEM

Learning to take good notes is an important technique to acquire. You will find that many courses do not have textbooks assigned for purchase. For these classes you will have to depend on the notes you take in class and in the library for most of the information you will study from for your examinations. Many professors give outlines of the course to their students, but many do not. You must take notes in class in either case.

You also have to take notes when you are reading material that has been assigned to you and when reading material for papers and projects. What do you write down when you write your notes?

Recognizing Main Points

One very important thing is that you don't write everything down. You must have the objective of writing down the facts you will need to use later, the points that the professor or author has made, and specific ideas and definitions. If you try to write everything down, you will find that you do not understand what you are writing, and you will not understand it later. Notes that were not clear when they were written will turn to pure mud later.

A trick I have developed over the years which has proved to be invaluable is learning to write without looking at what I have written. You miss a great deal when you have to take your eyes off the speaker and the blackboard to look at your paper. No one is going to have to read your notes but yourself. With some practice, you will find that you can write fairly straight and that you will be able to judge when you have reached the edge of the page.

Outlining Notes

When you are taking notes, you need to think about what you will be using those notes for in the future. If you are going to study from those notes, you should put them in outline form. Begin with the main idea of the class or the topic. Make subheadings under the main heading. You may want to include specific names, dates, and definitions. Are there phrases you may need to use to answer questions at a later date? If you listen carefully during a lecture, you can often identify potential questions which may appear on exams at a later date. Make a little note to yourself about those possible questions and their answers. You will find them helpful when you are studying the material. Whatever you do, don't write down everything you hear. It will be confusing. (It may also be boring).

If you are taking notes on material you are reading for a paper or project, you may have to use a slightly different approach. You will not get any clues from the teacher as to the comparative importance of different sections. If you have already outlined your paper, you will have some idea of the material you need. One technique is to prepare the basic outline for the paper first and then either number or name the different sections of the paper. As you read your material, you will be able to identify the notes you are writing with the different sections of your paper.

Do not write your notes one after the other, but put them on separate sheets of paper or on cards. Do not put writing on both sides of the sheet. You can spend endless amounts of time turning sheets of paper over looking for some piece of information that you remember writing but can't find. When you are assembling the final draft of your paper, you may want to go to a "cut and paste" technique as I do. Never write a piece of rough copy over when you can cut and paste it together for your final typing. Remember that you are trying to save yourself time and effort. You cannot do this if you have written your notes on both sides of the page. Mark your notes with the numbers and/or section names from your paper outline. If you have not designed the full outline when you start your paper, you can still use key words at the top of the card or sheet so you will be able to identify the information easily.

When you have completed your research, you will be able to group the cards according to section numbers or key words.

If you do not need the exact words of the author, try to summarize them in phrases that may be useful to you later. Be certain that you have the exact reference indicated. I put the reference on a separate card and number it. When I make a note of what the author said, I don't have to put the total reference down each time. The cards which carry the complete reference are then useful when I am putting together the bibliography.

If you find that you need the exact words of the author or if there is a table or a great deal of information to be copied, make use of the copying machine.

You may find that you are working for twenty cents an hour, laboriously copying out material by hand.

Revising the Outline

Once you have done the major part of your research, you can arrange the cards or the sheets of paper by topic according to the outline. You may have found material that you cannot use and you may have some "holes" in your notes. Write your paper according to the original outline or a revised outline. Always remember that your work must have a point of focus. Don't include something from your notes just because you have written it down and don't want to waste it.

You also need to achieve a balance in your project. You should have more material to support your main points than your secondary points. The material supporting the main points should be substantial. If this is not the case, consider revising your outline. You may need to do this anyway after you have done your research. You must sometimes be willing to make this decision.

Your notes are for your use. Experiment with the format, the material (paper, cards, ink, pencil) until you have a system of note-taking that works best for you.

FOOTNOTES AND BIBLIOGRAPHY

Avoiding Plagiarism

While you are doing the research for your papers and projects, you will find yourself reading many books and papers. The importance of giving full credit to authors not only for specific statements but also for essential ideas cannot be stressed too strongly. You will be aware if you are using a direct quotation. The question which requires some real "soul searching" occurs with the need for referencing ideas. During the course of your reading, you will absorb and perhaps modify some general ideas. You may also be re-reporting the ideas of others pretty directly. When in doubt, give a reference, is a rule which I use. Plagiarism is a situation that has caused trouble for many students and reduced their image in the eyes of the institution. It may also cause you to fail a course or be put on probation. Be aware of what you are doing.

When you are giving an indication that you have taken either an exact quotation from someone or have taken information or ideas from someone, you will have to give a footnote for that information. You may reference the idea in the text in a number of ways, such as: "Henry Jones reports that the ZMW atom will melt at 380°," "Sam Hinkelmeyer discusses the theory in a number of articles," "Patricia Moser stresses this viewpoint in her latest book." In each of these cases you would not have quotation marks in your paper (they appear here to let you know that they are examples). You would have to give a footnote to let the reader know where he or she could find the material.

Footnote Format

Footnotes are little blocks of information that tell the reader where to go to get the original piece of work. They may also contain additional information or remarks. This latter technique is used by some researchers but it should generally be avoided by the beginning report writer. The footnote, if it is to be useful, must contain the following information: The name of the author, authors or editor of the book or article, the title of the work, the year of publication and publishing company with the city of publication. In the case of a magazine or journal, the title of the journal, the volume, and issue number must be included.

There are many types of references which do not fit this pattern, such as dissertations, audiovisual materials, conversations with noted individuals, and paintings. There are certain formats for listing this type of material which may differ slightly from one subject matter to another or from one school to another. The basic format for the footnote may be presented in a slightly different manner. These specifications will be set out in the style manual which may be recommended by your school.

Let me give you some examples of the manner in which a reference to a book may differ. First of all you may put the footnote on the page where the reference occurs, in which case you put a little number above the line at the reference and a corresponding number at the bottom of the page at the place you give the footnote information. You start your series of numbers over again with each page. Usually the footnote is indented five or six spaces. Alternatively, the footnotes for a chapter may be grouped at the end of a chapter or may be at the end of the book. The numbering of the footnotes in the chapter of the book would proceed accordingly. Sometimes the last name of the author, separated by a comma from the first name, is the first entry in the footnote. Other formats use different arrangements.

The bibliography is a list of all the books and reference materials that are used in your paper. The materials are listed alphabetically and there are no page numbers included, generally. There are different approved formats for bibliographies also.

Find the style manual, or see what is acceptable for your school or profession, and make out a sample card for a book and for a magazine or journal bibliography entry. Keep this card with you when you are doing your research work. Every time you take down the reference information, take down the complete information in the correct order and in the proper form. If you have some file cards with you, put each reference on a separate card. You can also make some notes about the reference on the same card. When you are selecting the final references, you can simply select the ones you want to use from the cards you have collected. To put your bibliography in alphabetical order, you simply put the cards in alphabetical order.

Some examples of footnote and bibliography format are given below.

Footnote:

[1] Karen Wolfe, *"Power Helps Analyze Electric Bills,"* BYTE, 4:10, October 1979, p. 48.

Bibliography:

Christopher, Matt. *Touchdown for Tommy.* Little, Brown and Company. Boston: 1959.

Please remember that the examples given are just that, examples. They are not models for you to copy.

If you do not have to use a set format, you can use these. You will find that different formats use commas, periods, and colons in different places and may also underline different things. Book titles are usually underlined but it is the volume number that is underlined more often than the title of a magazine or the title of the article. Make the file card with your format on it for your use.

TYPE THE PAPER

No matter what you have to do to get a paper typed, do it. It is important that you act as though you know what going to college is all about. One thing that students are expected to know is that papers must be typed.

It is impossible for professors to read handwritten papers. You want to put your reader in a good mood when he or she is going to give you a grade. Many professors will refuse to accept the paper and may even give you a failing grade on the report if it is handwritten. Some will give you a reduced grade. Others may not say that they are giving you a reduced grade, but they will be doing it subconsciously if not consciously.

Keep It Neat

I have also seen students reduce their chance of a higher grade in order to save a few cents. I cannot think of any other reason but economy for students to single space a paper or write it from edge to edge of the paper. Double space and use decent margins. Be sure of spelling and grammar. Proofread your work. Make the headings consistent and use a dark ribbon. The proper presentation will enhance your grade and indicate to the professor that you care about your work.

If you can scrape together the money, get an electric typewriter. It will make typing easier for you even if you are already a good typist. Learn to type your own papers. You will still be ahead of the game, rather than paying someone and having to give them the material far in advance of the deadline. Remember that you are trying to balance your time and energy. The more independent you are, the more efficiently you can operate. Make your work clean and neat, use erasable bond if necessary, and don't forget to double space your paper.

Keep A Copy

One other thing that you mustn't forget is to make a copy of your work. Never give the professor the only copy of your paper. Most colleges have a copier in the library or perhaps in the department office. The five or ten cents a page you may have to pay will be well worth it if the paper should be lost. Also, you may want a copy of your paper that is free from teacher comments. The comments may be useful or you may not agree with them. It is handy to have both copies of the paper in your file.

Keep A File

Do keep a file of your papers. It is possible to use the research done in one course as a beginning for research in another course. I am not suggesting that a paper be used for more than one assignment, but you may need to use references again. You will also be able to profit from reviewing the comments made on one paper when you are beginning another one.

Epilogue

Returning to school is a thing you will do with both joy and fear. Try to spend the time working and not worrying. Be efficient, but spend time talking with students as a part of learning.

Use these years to develop yourself. Include your family, look to the future, but live in the present.

Above all, be ready, good luck, and have a good time.

INDEX

Index

A

B

C

R

S

T

V